S0-ARW-526

TIPS
FOR THE BUSINESS TRAVELER
—— IN ASIA ——

TIPS

FOR THE BUSINESS TRAVELER
——— IN ASIA ———

Practical advice on 10 Asian countries
for the independent business traveler. From the
editors of Asian Sources Books, in association with
TRAVELER magazine.

THE ASM GROUP

Publications
of The Asian Sources
Media Group

From the same publishers:

Importing From China
Importing From Hong Kong
Importing From India
Importing From Korea
Importing From Malaysia
Importing From Taiwan
Importing From Thailand
Importing From The Philippines
Importing From Singapore
Importing From Vietnam
Importing From China (in Japanese)
Importing From Taiwan (in Japanese)

Importing From Czechoslovakia
Importing From Mexico
Importing From Poland
Negotiating in Asia

Every effort has been made to check the facts and figures to ensure the accuracy of this manual; however, the publishers do not accept responsibility for errors or omissions.

No part of this work may be reproduced or copied in any form by any means — graphics, electronic or mechanical, including photocopying, recording, taping or information and retrieval systems — without written permission of the publisher.

This edition published in 1992
© 1992 Trade Media Ltd.
All rights reserved
ISBN 962-7138-25-8

Printed by
Allion Printing Co. Ltd.
Hong Kong

CONTENTS

Business hours ▪ Communications ▪ Currency ▪
Entertainment, eating out and night life ▪
Electricity ▪ Geography and climate ▪ Language
and people ▪ Local time ▪ Medical care ▪ Name
cards ▪ Newspapers ▪ Radio and television ▪ Public
holidays ▪ Shopping ▪ Silence routine ▪ Tipping ▪
Travelers checks and credit cards ▪ A brief history ▪
Diplomatic missions abroad

Taiwan ■ Getting around Taiwan ■ Getting around major cities ■ Taxis ■ Rent a car ■ Accommodation ■ Physical exercise facilities ■ Entertainment ■ Night life ■ Climate ■ Currency and credit ■ Name cards ■ Tipping ■ Dress ■ Business hours ■ Medical care ■ Vaccinations ■ Public holidays ■ Local time ■ A brief history of Taiwan and its people ■ Telecommunications ■ Taiwan addresses overseas

INTRODUCTION

Business travel in Asia can be a delight. Or it can be stressful, expensive and uncomfortable. The difference often can be traced to the expectations of the traveler and how prepared he or she is for what they encounter.

While many bookstores sell travel books primarily aimed at tourists, publications that carry information aimed specifically at the independent business traveler are few and far between.

Tips for the Business Traveler in Asia — written by business travelers for business travelers — meets this specific information need. It contains data that is practical and useful to the first time business visitor to Asia, as well as to the frequent business traveler. Combining essential information with the insights of experienced travelers this book covers 10 Asian countries.

A concise, easy to read publication, it is designed to help you navigate the contrasting travelling environments of China, Hong Kong, India, Korea, Malaysia, the Philippines, Singapore, Taiwan, Thailand, and Vietnam.

It has been researched and written by staff writers of the Asian Sources Media Group, whose trade magazines have been covering business across Asia for over 20 years, and by the *Traveler* magazine staff, whose monthly publication provides up-to-date information about Asia for the independent business traveler.

We take you from the luxury of Singapore's Changi airport to the spartan streets of Hanoi, and tell the best way to get to your business destinations in both cities. We tell you about taxis and local transportation in several Asian cities and how to get safe rides at a fair price. We tell you about local customs and how to avoid offending your hosts. And much more: insider's tips about visa applications, accommodation, communications, business hours, appropriate attire; information on climate, geography, holidays and history. We also include a list of key overseas government contacts at the end of each chapter, to help you make your business plans before you set out to Asia.

Of course, this book cannot take away the stress and frustration of the unexpected. But, it will allow you to be better prepared for your business travel to Asia by letting you know what to expect. This in itself makes this book a valuable part of the preparation for your next business trip to the fastest growing economic region of the world.

ACKNOWLEDGEMENTS

Asian Sources Books and *Traveler* magazine wish to thank the following people for researching this book: Lina Goh, Stuart Hampton, Chris Hanrahan, Tony Howlett, Bruce Humes, Sarah McDonald, Eric Mueller, M. Raghu Ram, Susan Pe and Caroline Robertson.

Special thanks are due to M. Raghu Ram, Stuart Hampton and Eric Mueller for editing, and to Amy Chiu and Gofanda Cheung for production and artwork assistance.

Trade Media Limited, 1992

C H A P T E R

CHINA

1

Visas ■ Passing places into and out of China ■ Air travel within China ■
Rail ■ Taxis ■ Buses ■ Hotels ■ Business hours ■ Climate ■ Currency ■
Customs procedures ■ Dress ■ Electricity supply ■ Gifts ■ Health ■
Holidays ■ Language ■ Local time ■ Name cards ■ Night life ■ The
people ■ Surveillance ■ Taiwan ■ Travelers checks and credit cards ■
Tipping ■ Selected list of government contacts overseas

CHINA

MOST MAJOR AIRLINES fly into Beijing, China's capital and a convenient city for access to the industrial heartland of China's northeast. From Beijing, Tianjin is a little over 100 km away, Dalian not much further and Shanghai just over two hours away by air. A few international flights fly direct to Shanghai.

Hong Kong's bustling international Kai Tak airport is the gateway to the south and is within easy reach of Guangdong province by air, as well as by rail and road. Macau, another stepping stone into China, is less than an hour away by jetfoil but is planned to have an airport in 1992. Guangzhou is also only three hours away by train. China's own airline, originally known as CAAC, but now broken up into smaller, competing firms, including Air China (for international services), has regular flights to many Chinese cities from Hong Kong, as does DragonAir. Hong Kong's airline, Cathay Pacific, has flights to Beijing and Shanghai.

There is also the rail route from Europe on the Trans-Siberian Express.

VISAS

All foreigners require a visa to enter China (those from South Africa, Israel or South Korea may have trouble getting one). These are issued by Chinese embassies and consulates in most countries. Nationals of countries where China has no diplomatic representation can apply for their visas from other countries or through the Visa Office of the Ministry of Foreign Affairs of the PRC in Hong Kong.

The correct procedure is first to make your contact with the PRC body you are dealing with, inside or outside China, and your contact will organize an invitation from an authorized body. This invitation, which is officially required for your business visa, will be communicated to the visa-issuing office.

This process can take a few weeks. If you are in Hong Kong and need to make an unscheduled visit in a hurry, there is another way round this — go on a tourist visa obtainable within a day at the China Travel Service (CTS). Tourist visas are valid for three months and to have them processed in one day costs HK$300; for a two-day wait, applications cost HK$200 and three-day ones, HK$150. They can be obtained at any one of the following CTS offices in Hong Kong:

4th Floor
78-83 Connaught Road Central
Central, Hong Kong
Tel: 853-3888

2nd Floor
77 Queens Road Central
Central, Hong Kong
Tel: 525-2284

1st Floor
27-33 Nathan Road
Tsimshatsui, Kowloon
Hong Kong
Tel: 721-1331

This is not the approved method, however, so the correct way should be tried first before attempting it. Should you have to go into China on a tourist visa it is unlikely that you will ever be asked any questions as nobody seems to worry about it!

Since 1986, foreign investors, who comply with certain conditions, have been able to apply for visas at some major points of entry, such as Beijing, Shanghai and Guangzhou. You can ask for full details of this at your nearest Chinese embassy or consulate.

If you have made your application, become anxious about the time it is taking to process and begin making inquiries at the Chinese visa-issuing office, insist on obtaining the name of the person who is following up on the progress of your application. That way, you can ask to talk to that person directly the next time that you call, for invariably you will be involved in more calls, involving possibly a bureaucratic merry-go-round. Also, your application will take much longer to obtain approval if you have to go through the same explanation with several different people each time you phone.

A standard visa is valid for only one journey into and out of China. However, visas for multiple visits are now available to businessmen from some locations. Make sure, though, that your planned lengths of stay will not make you eligible to pay income tax to the Chinese authorities.

PASSING PLACES INTO AND OUT OF CHINA

Officially approved in 1986 were 71 "passing places" through which

Chinese and foreigners can enter and leave China. There are now 436 open cities and counties in China to which foreigners may travel freely without having to apply for travel permits. Outside the open cities permission is required from the Public Security Bureau. There is more chance of this being granted if permission is sought in a major center rather than a small local office. Details can be obtained from your local Chinese embassy.

AIR TRAVEL WITHIN CHINA

The official Chinese airline, CAAC (or its announced successor for international flights, Air China) has had its monopoly on domestic flights diluted by some official regional services such as Oriental Airlines (Shanghai), Southwest Airlines (Chengdu) and, in future, Xian, Shenyang and Guangzhou. However, domestic air travel is not without its difficulties.

Many travelers return from the PRC with scare stories about low levels of safety, particularly about the age and type of aircraft (often old Soviet turbo-prop) in the Chinese fleet, cabin instructions and airport approach procedures.

Although many of the tales are clearly subjective and sometimes exaggerated, you have to go a long way to find any foreigner who would prefer not to go by domestic aircraft if there was a choice.

The Chinese safety record, with, for example, no casualties in 1987, would appear to contradict those fears. However, a bad crash early in 1988 brought a statement from the government which condemned the lack of safety levels, grounded many of the older aircraft for checks and urged the airline to invest in modern aircraft. There are already some small jet planes in service and more up-to-date larger aircraft have been bought. The government is so sensitive about complaints that it seems likely the problems will be sorted out in the long term.

Meanwhile, with an insufficient number of aircraft to meet the demand for seats on its major routes, and with any checks or repairs reducing the numbers available at any given time, schedules are often changed and flights canceled or postponed for many hours without notice. It is not uncommon for travelers to be left stranded or delayed without having the benefit of an announcement. The schedules can also be thrown out by bad weather, which prevents pilots from making the visual approach necessary to land at many of the smaller airports since these do not have any radar systems. While Beijing's air control is more sophisticated and is under improvement, delays at other airports can have a knock-on effect.

Because of the uncertainty which often attends domestic air travel, those working from resident offices who have to travel constantly within China prefer to take a "soft-sleeper" train. However, the journeys are often too long to be practicable and the standards, vastly different from Western trains, coupled with potential language difficulties, make this form of transport inadvisable.

The other major snag regarding air travel is making a booking. The Chinese system is not yet fully computerized, making it necessary to book several days in advance. It is unwise to attempt this yourself unless your hotel has a travel desk. If there is one, give yourself plenty of time and make your booking at least three days before the day you wish to leave — but be prepared to surrender your passport for that period while the ticket is being processed. If there is a change of plans at the last minute or if it is impossible for you to wait that long, then it is best to throw yourself at the mercy of your PRC contact.

Even if you do not have a hotel travel desk, your contact will usually expect, in any case, to be asked to make the travel arrangements for you. The alternative — wrestling through a melee of administrative confusion at a local CAAC office — is not something you will relish, even if you have the time at your disposal.

Booking domestic flights from Hong Kong will not speed up the process. There will still be a delay of several days before any ticket can be confirmed because of the need to wait for a reply after your travel agent has sent a fax or telex to the central booking office in China.

The aircraft are often fully booked even though there is not a full passenger complement. This appears to be in case senior officials show up unexpectedly at the last minute and have to be accommodated. Sometimes it is possible to persuade the airline to give up one of the vacant seats (if they exist). It has been known, too, on occasion, for a native Chinese passenger to be removed from his seat to make way for a foreigner. If this happens to you, you will have to make up your own mind if you can accept this.

Despite all these potential problems it is nevertheless quite possible to have trouble-free domestic air travel. Besides, you will usually have no other choice.

There are many plans for new airports and for improvements to existing ones. However, because these are changed so often, it is unwise to plan future trips around the possibilities of such plans coming to fruition in time for when you are required to make your business trips.

RAIL

If you are looking for an experience, have time to spare, or are squeamish at the thought of domestic flights, rail travel is worth considering. It is cheap, but by no means comfortable.

To be avoided are "hard" seats. The description sums up the seats perfectly but does not even begin to describe the primitive conditions surrounding them, aggravated by the inevitable language difficulties, despite the usual friendliness of your fellow passengers. On long journeys, the only option is a "soft sleeper" (a "hard" bed is virtually out of the question). Carriage compartments are shared by four passengers; the faces may change constantly on long journeys. If the guard can speak your language, a journey may become tolerable. If not, you will encounter difficulties in obtaining a seat during the short occasions the refreshments car is open and problems in ordering food. By Western standards the eating experience is a little squalid. To fortify themselves against the cold during winter or against the boredom, many Chinese take a dosage of their favorite liquor along with them. Do not be surprised if you are offered to share some, but be prepared for the fire in the throat.

The Chinese take mugs with them for filling with tea from a communal pot of hot water.

Booking is best done through your Chinese contact or a hotel travel desk. If you do it yourself beware of the shake of the head; during busy times — when the Guangzhou trade fair is being held, for example — the clerk may tell you there are no seats left. A ticket for a seat, nevertheless, may be available from the hotel next door, or even at the original clerk's desk if you go back within half an hour.

Finding your way to the correct train is easy at Guangzhou, difficult at most of the other stations, where Chinese are often waiting in hundreds for a chance to get a ticket, sometimes for days, even in the harshest of weather. Foreigners usually do not have the same trouble in obtaining tickets and may be shown a different way through the station concourse to avoid the crowds. The date, and carriage and seat numbers are on the ticket in Chinese. It is advisable to check and recheck what they are while purchasing the ticket.

TAXIS

Very few locations, such as Guangzhou, have a plentiful supply of taxis that can be hailed from the street in the normal fashion. They are scarce in many areas. There should be no problem in Beijing if you take a taxi from your hotel; trying to stop one in the street is virtually impossible. Outside Guangzhou it is advisable, and not expensive, to hire a taxi for a morning or a day. Fares vary from place to place. Beijing is one of the cheapest locations, Guangzhou one of the more expensive. Allow yourself plenty of time for visits in cities such as Shanghai, which is highly congested. Taxi drivers carry a receipt book and they will issue receipts automatically in cities such as Beijing, but you have to ask in Guangzhou. It is a good idea to make sure one is issued. Payment is by foreign exchange certificate (*see later section on Other Tips, Currency*).

Most taxi drivers do not speak English. It is advisable to have the addresses of the places that you are going to visit written down in Chinese before you go to China or when you are in China by one of the hotel staff. Even then, the driver may have difficulty in finding the address, because of the numbering system adopted in some locations.

BUSES

Apart from the ubiquitous bicycle, many Chinese travel by local buses, which are, therefore, often crowded. Destinations are in Chinese, as are the announcements of them, which are either shouted out or given over a loudspeaker system by the driver. Not recommended for the fleeting business visitor.

HOTELS

Many hotels are joint ventures with foreign companies and are up to international standards (including price), with the usual facilities, such as business centers, often with a fax service available. Many new hotels are being built — so many, in fact, that in some places construction has been called to a halt to prevent a glut. The Chinese have their own hotels, too, but the standards of these vary. Many of these are called Friendship Hotels, and although they are not up to international standards and have a limited choice of food, they are cheaper. Payment for some items, such as room service, if it is available, may be demanded on the spot (or at least separately) by the floor clerk when you are checking out. Hotel rules are strict, right down to smoking in bed, which is forbidden. One foreigner who ignored this regulation and started a fire, which turned out to be lethal, was jailed. Room guests are allowed within normal times. Be prepared for language difficulties.

China now has about 1,600 hotels, offering 250,000 rooms, of which some 10 percent are rated deluxe. The best (and the biggest choice) of these are in the areas spearheading the country's export drive. The largest foreign hotel group operating in China is Holiday Inn Asia-Pacific, which plans to have 20 hotels open throughout the country by 1995. Bookings can be made from any of its hotels throughout the world through Holidex II, the largest privately-owned computerized reservation system anywhere.

BUSINESS HOURS

The Chinese work a six-day week, usually from 8 am to 6 pm, with a lunch break of 90 minutes to two hours from about 11.30 am or noon. Offices are generally closed on Sundays.

CLIMATE

China's vast geographical size is matched by the differences in its climate. The differences are most marked in winter, when in the north the temperatures can plummet to -40C, while the extreme south experiences a more sub-tropical environment. Summer in the north is often hot and humid. In the south, it is hotter and wetter.

CURRENCY

Foreigners are supposed to use Foreign Exchange Certificates (FECs) rather than the renminbi (Rmb) used by Chinese citizens. This policy is enforced by the restaurants, hotels, Friendship Stores, shops and taxis catering to foreigners. The certificates are obtainable from hotel exchange counters, Bank of China branches, or from branches of foreign banks, in denominations of 50, 10, 5 and 1 yuan, and 5 and 1 jiao. Premises not normally catering to foreigners will accept Rmb if you have any, but may not accept FECs. Rmb may be given as change in some cases, but bear in mind that if you do acquire any, you are not allowed to take it out of China. In cities like Shanghai, foreigners are often approached by Chinese offering good exchange rates for foreign money in exchange for Rmb. This is illegal and should be avoided. There is little to be gained as most purchases or bills can be settled with FECs.

At Shenzhen, on the border with Hong Kong, most bills are quoted in Hong Kong dollars, but FECs are accepted. To avoid confusion, it is best to try to make clear the currency that you are offering before the bill is brought or while making a purchase.

CUSTOMS PROCEDURES

Currency and some specific items such as cameras, wristwatches, calculators and portable computers, have to be declared on arrival. Failure to do so may mean difficulty in getting the equipment out again, since the original declaration has to be shown on departure. If a valuable item such as a camera does 'go missing' (nothing ever actually gets 'stolen' in China), it is important that you file a report with the nearby police. Failure to do so could mean that you might have to pay import duty when you leave.

DRESS

For formal occasions a suit and tie are expected, but generally dress is informal. The usual advice is to wear what would be expected for the occasion in your own country.

ELECTRICITY SUPPLY

China's domestic supply is 220V at 50Hz. If you intend to use an appliance in a hotel, such as a portable computer, a variety of socket types may be encountered, even within one room. Use of an appliance, such as an iron, requires the hotel's permission, at least in theory. If you like to read, take two 100 watt bulbs with you — one with bayonet base and one with screw base.

GIFTS

There are strict rules governing the acceptance of gifts from foreigners to PRC personnel. The Chinese are not officially allowed to take a gift, unless it is forced upon them, in which case they are supposed to turn it over to the authorities. The wording of the regulations is ambiguous, however. If you are intent on giving a present to your contact, bear in mind that if he is not the top man, or influential, his acceptance of your gift may be frowned upon by his superiors.

HEALTH

Visitors to China have to sign a health declaration on entry. If the visitor has come from an area where there are diseases such as cholera or yellow fever, he may be required to have a vaccination certificate.

Once in China, it is not advisable to drink tap water. Most joint venture hotels have a doctor on call. Foreigners can generally expect the best medical treatment available if it is required. Many hospitals have a special ward for them. Anyone with a regular need for a specific medication should bring it along. Prescriptions made out in China may involve either Chinese or Western medicines.

Rabies is present. An animal bite should not be ignored; go immediately to a doctor.

HOLIDAYS

There are seven public holidays:

New Year's Day	January 1
Spring Festival — Three days	January or
(Chinese or Lunary New Year)	February (variable)
International Labor Day	May 1
National Day	October 1 and 2

LANGUAGE

The national language is known in the West as Mandarin, and in China as *putonghua*. While there are many local dialects, the written language is unchanged from area to area (but slightly different in Hong Kong and Taiwan). Romanization is only an approximation; two systems are used, Wade-Giles and *pinyin*, the latter is seen more commonly, such as in street names and railway stations.

LOCAL TIME

All China is based on Beijing time, which is the same as Hong Kong time. This is eight hours ahead of GMT, apart from May through September, when it is seven hours ahead. It is 13 hours ahead of Eastern Standard Time.

NAME CARDS

It is the norm to exchange name cards with everyone you meet on official (and often unofficial) business. This can come to four or five people at each meeting. You should go armed with at least 100. Printing services are easily available in Hong Kong, and at some of the joint venture hotels.

NIGHT LIFE

There is not much night life unless you can find a watering hole frequented by resident foreign businessmen or are being accompanied by a local Chinese prepared to give you a glimpse of the sparse entertainment available. Be prepared for long evenings outside of those that are taken up with the occasional dinner banquet.

THE PEOPLE

Fifty-five races make up the population, dominated by the Han Chinese (94 percent), who live in less than half of the geographical area of the PRC. The 54 minority nationalities, living in the rest of the country (mainly the north, northwest and the mountains), are distinct from the Han in many ways, such as their histories, languages and customs. The Zhuang, at about 13 million, make up the largest group.

As the areas inhabited by the minorities are mainly in the autonomous regions (ARs), the ARs have additional responsibilities toward them and over their relationship, sometimes uneasy, with the Han.

SURVEILLANCE

Are the movements of foreigners watched closely by the Chinese authorities? Most regular visitors to China agree that the answer is probably "No", although comings and goings at the hotel are monitored. Some businessmen are a little nervous about sending telexes as copies are taken and are, presumably, gathered at some collection point. It seems hardly likely, however, that somebody goes through the hundreds of telexes to gather business intelligence for use against a buyer.

TAIWAN

Taiwan is regarded by the Chinese as one of its provinces, even though Taiwan (which calls itself the Republic of China and also considers itself a Chinese province), does not accept rule from the mainland. Reference to Taiwan as a separate country is likely to cause offense in China.

TRAVELERS CHECKS AND CREDIT CARDS

Most well-known travelers' checks are accepted throughout China. Credit cards are widely accepted, particularly in the places that foreigners frequent.

TIPPING

Tips are, in theory, forbidden in China, whether they be for taxis, a waiter or the hotel porter. In practice, it depends where you are. The staff at hotels in Beijing, for example, must not accept a tip. If they do, they will be punished. Taxi drivers there do not expect one. As you get closer to Hong Kong, however, tipping becomes more acceptable. Western-style hotels and taxi drivers in Guangzhou or Shenzhen, for instance, will readily take a tip, just like anywhere else in the world. For the moment, the best policy is not to tip in case of giving offense, at least outside Guangzhou.

SELECTED LIST OF GOVERNMENT CONTACTS OVERSEAS
Economic and Commercial Organizations:

ASIA

India
PRC Commercial Office
50-D Shantipath
Chanakyapuri
New Delhi 110 021
India
Tel: 608944, 600328
Tlx: 3166250 SINO IN
Cable: CHINEMB NEW DELHI

Japan
PRC Commercial Office
16-8 Minami-Azabu 5-chome
Minato-ku 106
Tokyo
Japan
Tel: (03) 440 2011
Tlx: CHICOTEL J28506
Fax: (03) 446 8242

Korea
PRC Commercial Office
Hong Mei Dong
Mao Laang Bong District Pyongyang
Korea
Tel: 390276, 390275
Cable: 0794

Malaysia
PRC Commercial Office
No. 34, 34A & 35B
Jalan Chan Chin Mooi
Setapak
Kuala Lumpur
Malaysia
Tel: 4239939, 4239937, 4239940
Tlx: CHIEMC MA 33675

Pakistan
PRC Commercial Office
43-6-B Block 6
P. E. C. H. S. Karachi
Pakistan
Tel: 430594, 437894
Tlx: 24038 CHICO PK

Cable: CHINCOMOFF KARACHI

The Philippines
PRC Commercial Office
2038 Roxas Boulevard
Metro Manila
Philippines
P.O. Box 7430 Airmail Exchange
Office
Manila International Airport
3120 Philippines
Tel: 572555, 584636
Tlx: 27682 EPRCC PH
Cable: SINOCOMM MANILA

Singapore
PRC Commercial Office
70-76 Dalvey Road
Singapore 1025
Tel: 7343360, 7343307
Tlx: RS 36878 CHICRO
Fax: 7338590
Cable: CHICOMER

Sri Lanka
PRC Commercial Office
45 Layards Road
Colombo 5
Tel: 580912
Tlx: 22408 CHINCO CE
Cable: CHINCOMOFF COLOMBO

Thailand
PRC Commercial Office
57 Rachad Apisake Road
Bangkok 10310
Thailand
Tel: 2457038, 245 7046
Cable: CHINAEMBA BANGKOK

Turkey
PRC Commercial Office
06700 Gaziosmanpasa Koroglu
Sokak No 72
Ankara
Turkey
Tel: 1377107
Tlx: 46387 CHCM TR

U.A.E.
PRC Commercial Office
Flat No. 1402
Khalifa Khandi Building
Corniche Road
Abu Dhabi
U.A.E.

AFRICA

Egypt
PRC Commercial Office
22 Bahgat Aly Street
Zamalek Cairo
Egypt
Tel: 417423, 416561
Tlx: 93180 CHICO UN CAIRO
Cable: CHINCOMOFF CAIRO

Kenya
PRC Commercial Office
Woodlands Road
Kilimani District
Nairobi Kenya
P.O. Box 48190 Nairobi
Tel: 721434
Tlx: 23011 CECOM KE
Cable: CHINAEMBA NAIROBI

Zimbabwe
PRC Commercial Office
10 Cork Road
Harare
Zimbabwe
P.O. Box 40 Harare
Tel: 730516
Tlx: 2569 CHINEB ZW OR 2310
XINHUA ZW
Cable: CHINCOM HARARE

EUROPE

Austria
PRC Commercial Office

1030 Wien Metternichgasse 4
Austria
Tel: 0222/753140
Tlx: 135794 CHINB A
Fax: 0043 222 7136816
Cable: CHINAEMBA WIEN

Belgium
PRC Commercial Office
21 Boulevard General Jacques
1050 Bruxelles
Belgique
Tel: (02) 6404006, 6404210
Tlx: 23328 AMCHIN B
Cable: AMBACHIN BRUXELLES

Britain
PRC Commercial Office
56-60 Lancaster Gate
London W2 3NG
Britain
Tel: (01) 262 0253
Cable: CHINACOM LONDON

Czechoslovakia
PRC Commercial Office
Majakovskeho 22
125, 26 Praha 6
Bubenec
Ceskoslovensko
Czechoslovakia
P.O. Box 125 26 Praha 6-Bubenec
Tel: 326143, 326141
Tlx: 121417 CHIEM-C
Cable: CHINAEMBA PRAHA

Denmark
PRC Commercial Office
Oregards Alle 12,2900
Hellerup Copenhagen
Denmark
Tel: (01) 611013
Tlx: 19106 CNCOEM DK
Cable: CHINAEMBA
COPENHAGEN

Germany
PRC Commercial Office

Friedrich-Ebert-Str 59 5300
Bonn-Bad Godesberg
Tel: 0228 353654, 353622, 353628
Tlx: 885672 VRCHH D

France
PRC Commercial Office
21 Rue De L'Amiral D'Estaing
75016 Paris
France
Tel: 47208682, 47206395
Tlx: 6649492 F SINOCOMF
Cable: SINOCOM CHVLY PARIS

Greece
PRC Commercial Office
No. 7 Diadochou Pavlou P.PSY
Chikon Athens 15452
P.O. Box 65188 Athens
Tel: 672381
Tlx: 226848 CPRC GR
Cable: CHINAEMBA ATHENS

Hungary
PRC Commercial Office
1068 Budapest VI
Benczur UTCA
17 Hungary
Tel: 225242, 224872
Tlx: 227733 CHIBE H
Cable: SINOEMB BUDAPEST

Italy
PRC Commercial Office
Via Della Camilluccia 613 00315
Roma
Italy
Tel: (00396) 3287206, 3284254
Tlx: 622162 CINACI
Cable: CHINACOM ROME

Netherlands
PRC Commercial Office
Groothaesebroekseweg 2A 2243
Ea Wassenaar
The Netherlands
Tel: 0175 16050
Tlx: 31699 CHICO NL

Fax: 01751 11206

Norway
PRC Commercial Office
Inkognitogata 11
Oslo 2
Norway 0258
Tel: (2) 449638
Tlx: 71304 KINAH N
Cable: CHINEMB OSLO

Poland
PRC Commercial Office
Ul Bonifraterska 1,00-203
Warszawa
Poland
Tel: 313861, 313869
Tlx: 813589 CHINA PL
Cable: SINOEMBASSY WARSZAWA

Portugal
The Commercial Office
Rua Antonio De Saldanha
42 1400 Lisboa Portugal
Tel: 611947
Tlx: 13274 CNCOM P

Spain
PRC Commercial Office
Arturo Soria 111
28043 Madrid
Espana
Tel: 413 5892, 413 2776
Tlx: 22808 EMCHI E

Sweden
PRC Commercial Office
Ringvagen 56
S-181 34 Lidingo
Sweden
Tel: 08 7674083, 7679625
Tlx: 16490 CHINO S
Fax: 56 08 7318404
Cable: hoplazatine stockholm

Switzerland
PRC Commercial Office
7 J.V. Widmannstrasse

3074 Muri Bern
Switzerland
P.O. Box 3074 Muri
Tel: (031) 521401, 521402
Tlx: 912629 HBCN CH
Cable: CHICOMOFF BERN

AUSTRALASIA

Australia
PRC Commercial Office
14 Federal Highway
Watson Canberra
A.C.T. 2602
Australia
Tel: (062) 412449
Tlx: CHIEM AA 62489
Cable: CHINAEMBA CANBERRA

New Zealand
PRC Commercial Office
2-6 Glenmore Street
Wellington
New Zealand
Tel: 721383
Tlx: CHINEMB NZ 3843
Cable: CHINAEMBA WELLINGTON

THE AMERICAS

Argentina
PRC Commercial Office
La Pampa 4350 (1430)
Capital Federal Republica
Argentina
Tel: 510172, 514593
Tlx: 24977 OCECH AR
Cable: CHINAEMBA
BUENOSAIRES

Brazil
PRC Commercial Office
Shis QI II Conjunto 3
Casa 16 Lago Sul Brasilia-DF
Brazil

P.O. Box CEP 71600
Tel: (061) 2484582, 2481446
Tlx: (061) 4525 ERPC BR

Canada
PRC Commercial Office
511-515 St. Patrick Street
Ottawa Ontario
Canada K1N 5H3
P.O. Box 8935
Tel: (613) 2342718
Tlx: 053-3770 CHINAEMBA OTT
Cable: CHINAEMBA OTTAWA

Chile
PRC Commercial Office
Av Da Pedro De Valdivia 1032
Santiago
Chile
P.O. Box Casilla 3417
Tel: 2239988, 2232465
Tlx: 242190 SICOM CL
Cable: CHINAEMBA
SANTIAGODE CHILE

USA
PRC Commercial Office
2300 Connecticut Avenue
N.W. Washington DC 20008
Tel: (202) 3282520, 3282523,
3282525
Tlx: 440673 PRCCUI
Cable: CHINAEMBA
WASHINGTON DC

Venezuela
PRC Commercial Office
Quinta "La Majada" Calle San
Pedro Prados Del Este
P.O. Box Apartado 80520 Zonapostal
1080
Caracas Venezuela
Tel: 771415/978, 4864
Tlx: 29590 OCECH VC

C H A P T E R

HONG KONG

Visas ■ Transportation ■ Attire ■ Business hours ■ Climate ■ Communications ■ Currency ■ Dining ■ Face ■ *Fung Shui* ■ Gifts ■ Health ■ Holidays ■ Public holidays ■ Hotels ■ Local time ■ Media ■ Medical facilities ■ Name cards ■ Night life ■ Religion ■ Tipping ■ A brief history ■ Major Hong Kong government contacts overseas

HONG KONG

BUSINESS EXECUTIVES TRAVELING to Hong Kong for the first time will find getting to the British colony to be relatively easy. It is well serviced by 38 of the world's major airlines. However, it is a popular tourist as well as business destination, and certain routes are very busy, so it pays to book early.

In addition to its mercantile reputation, Hong Kong has also built up a flourishing tourist industry over the years. With its location as a gateway to China, its spectacular harbor, its "shopper's paradise" image and its vast array of leisure and entertainment activities, the business traveler can take advantage of all these attractions, as well as the sophisticated business networks that are in place.

VISAS

Visas are required only by nationals of former Eastern Bloc countries, (although plans are underway to relax these restrictions) and a few other places, such as Cuba, Cambodia, Laos and Vietnam. Visitors from all other countries do not require visas provided they have onward tickets. Permission to stay varies from seven days to three months according to nationality, although British passport holders can stay for up to six months. Applications for an extension of stay can be made at the Immigration Department. Those intending to travel frequently in and out of Hong Kong should apply for a multiple re-entry visa. Visitors can transact business during the stay, but the entry permit does not entitle the holder to take up residence, employment or establish a business in Hong Kong. Questions concerning visa requirements and status should be directed to your nearest British consular office.

TRANSPORTATION

An attractive feature of Hong Kong is its large network of harbor and island ferries, constantly sailing between Hong Kong Island, Kowloon, parts of the New Territories and the outlying islands. The Star Ferry, from 6.30 am to 11.30 pm daily, plies to and fro between Hong Kong Island and Tsimshatsui on the Kowloon side every few minutes (HK$1.20 for first class). The Mass Transit Railway (MTR) is the fastest way to commute between Kowloon and the Central District on Hong Kong Island, as well as providing a fast link to the factory areas of Kwun Tong and Tsuen Wan. The MTR runs from 6 am until 1 am the next day, and fares vary according to destination.

A new Eastern Harbour tunnel for the MTR and automotive traffic connecting Quarry Bay (on Hong Kong Island) to Lam Tin (in Kowloon) was opened in 1990. This cuts down time when commuting to Quarry Bay and Kwun Tong.

Taxis are plentiful in Hong Kong and fares are low by international standards, HK$8.00 (flag fall) for the first two kilometers and HK$1.10 cents for every 1/4-kilometer thereafter. There is a carrying surcharge of HK$2 for each piece of large luggage, a HK$10 fee for passing through the Cross Harbor Tunnel, and smaller fees for going through the territory's other tunnels. If you use a Hong Kong-based taxi rather than a Kowloon-based taxi to travel from Hong Kong to Kowloon you will have to pay double the harbor tunnel toll and *vice versa*. Waiting is charged at 90 cents for every two minutes.

It is generally wise to have one of the hotel staff write down any address you intend to visit in Chinese characters because many taxi drivers do not understand English particularly well.

Hong Kong also has a full complement of double-decker buses, minibuses and trams. Private cars can also be hired. The minibuses can be a little confusing as there are no defined stops, and you are expected to scream out instructions to the driver in Cantonese as you approach your destination to indicate where you want to get off. The trams offer a slow but relaxing way to view Hong Kong provided you do not intend to use them in the rush hour. There is a charge of HK$1 for any length of journey.

Some 38 major international airlines fly to Hong Kong, providing around 1,000 scheduled passenger services each week. Kai Tak Airport is one of the world's busiest, and is served by airport coach services, hotel buses, taxis and hire-cars. The taxi fare should be about HK$30 to HK$40 for a journey to the main hotel area of Tsimshatsui in Kowloon, and about HK$40 to HK$60 (including the Harbour Tunnel charge) to the north shore of Hong Kong Island. When leaving Hong Kong, an airport departure tax is levied at a rate of HK$150 per adult and HK$50 per child under 12. Hong Kong is a tax-free port and only six groups of commodities — tobacco, alcoholic liquors, hydrocarbons, methyl alcohol, cosmetics and nonalcoholic beverages — are subject to excise duty. The duty is generally low. Nonresidents are allowed to bring into Hong Kong, duty free, a one-liter bottle of alcohol together with 200 cigarettes (or 50 cigars or 250 grams of tobacco); 60 milliliters of perfume and 250 milliliters of toilet water are also permitted.

ATTIRE

Business suits are generally worn all year round by government officials, bankers and executives of large companies, with casual attire the rule for factories.

BUSINESS HOURS

Banks
9.00 - 16.30 Mondays - Fridays
9.00 - 12.30 Saturdays

Government and business offices
8.30/9.00 - 13.00, 14.00 - 16.30/17.00/17.30
Mondays - Fridays
8.30/9.00 - 12.30/13.00
Saturdays

Shops
10.30 - 21.30 (hours may vary)
Most shops are open seven days a week.

Many factories take lunch from 12 and 1 o'clock, work a full day on Saturdays, and generally open for work earlier and close much later than other businesses.

CLIMATE

The subtropical climate makes Hong Kong very hot and humid during the April to September period with temperatures hovering around 30 degrees Celsius (around 90 degrees Fahrenheit). Approximately 80 percent of Hong Kong's annual rainfall occurs during this period. The winter months from October to March are generally pleasant with medium-cool evenings. Seldom does the temperature drop below 10 degrees Celsius (50 degrees Fahrenheit).

COMMUNICATIONS

Telephone calls within Hong Kong are free, but hotels do levy a small charge per call. Public telephones require a HK$1 coin. All telephone numbers were standardized to 7-digit numbers at the beginning of 1990 to reduce the confusion of area codes. Hotels can arrange long-distance phone calls, cables, telex and facsimile transmissions, as well as computer communications in many cases. IDD (International Direct Dialing) is available and fairly easily installed into homes and offices.

CURRENCY

The Hong Kong Dollar is the official currency and notes come in denominations of $10, $20, $50, $100, $500 and $1,000. Coins come in denominations of $5, $2, $1, 50 cents, 20 cents, and 10 cents. Exchange rates with leading foreign currencies are posted in hotels and banks. For many years, the value of the Hong Kong dollar has been tied to that of the U.S. dollar at a rate of about HK$7.80 to US$1.00.

Authorized money changers are located on just about every street in the main commercial areas and they offer better exchange rates than do the hotels (which charge a premium for the service) and the money changers at Kai Tak International Airport. However, many money changers charge a commission which more than offsets their better rates. Most banks also provide money-changing services. Foreign currencies can be freely exchanged without restriction, and currencies can be taken into and out of Hong Kong without restriction. Most major credit cards are widely accepted.

DINING

A good deal of Hong Kong's business is negotiated and finalized over meals and drinks. Public restaurants and private social clubs are preferred by Chinese for business dining and entertainment, and spouses seldom are included. Also, Chinese businessmen rarely invite foreigners, colleagues or clients to their homes.

Good food and atmosphere are considered essential, according to the Chinese, to form a suitable setting in which to conduct business. However, the popular Chinese *dim sum* lunch, where dishes are hawked to the various tables by trolley-pushing waitresses through extremely large, crowded and noisy restaurants, is not really conducive to conducting business in the Western sense.

Dinner is a different matter. Sooner or later you will be invited to an elaborate Chinese banquet featuring up to 12 or more courses accompanied by plenty of soft drinks, beer, cognac or scotch. It is

27

customary to toast each course as it is being served with the saying *Yam sing!* (Chinese equivalent to "Cheers!"). These feasts generally last two or more hours, sufficient to test your stamina. Mercifully, however, they usually break up immediately after the last course is served.

It is often a nice gesture to reciprocate, after being entertained at a Chinese banquet, by arranging a private dinner party for your Hong Kong supplier and some of his staff. The food and beverage manager at the hotel where you are staying can make all the arrangements. Both Western and Chinese meals can be ordered, though Western food is the common choice among businessmen of all nationalities.

FACE

The Chinese often attach embarrassment or "loss of face" to happenings different from those which would cause loss of dignity in the West. To avoid disrupting your business relationship and hurting someone's feelings unintentionally, do not deliberately make a Chinese look foolish and do not force a Chinese to admit outright that he has made a mistake or failed. If it is important to point out that an error has been made, do it without humiliating the person. Also, the Chinese may find it difficult to tell you that you are wrong.

FUNG SHUI

There are many ancient Chinese superstitions still prevalent today, and it is common for even the most modern Hong Kong businessman to consult with fortune tellers when selecting new premises or the site for a new factory. The direction of waterways, shapes of hills, heights and shapes of buildings, direction of roads, etc., all are said to have a bearing on whether good or evil spirits will affect the premises, and decisions are actually made depending on whether the *fung shui* is good or bad. Such considerations may not stand up to scientific scrutiny, but they can definitely affect property prices.

GIFTS

The giving of gifts is generally not expected in Hong Kong among businessmen. Employees are not allowed to accept gifts without approval from their managers, and the offering of gifts or incentives to government officials is against the law and policed by the Independent Commission Against Corruption (ICAC). Dinner parties are preferred instead of gifts. However, if you are intent on giving a gift, avoid giving a watch or clock, since Chinese superstition considers timepieces as unlucky business gifts, denoting a "count-down" toward death.

HEALTH

Cholera certificates are generally only required for individuals coming from an infected area. However, there are odd cases of cholera in Hong Kong from time to time, and anyone planning to travel in the East Asia region is advised to consult a doctor on necessary inoculation and vaccination. Yellow fever inoculation is needed only for travelers from countries where the disease is known to exist. Hong Kong has a few private hospitals where a visitor can receive treatment on a par with that in the West.

HOLIDAYS

There are 17 annual public holidays which combine both Western and Chinese customs. Government offices, banks and many commercial companies are closed on these days. However, factories commonly observe only the Chinese festivals which are based on the lunar calendar and vary from year to year. Those holidays are marked with an asterisk (*) on the table below, and the dates on which they fall in 1992 are indicated.

PUBLIC HOLIDAYS

New Year's Day	January 1
Chinese (Lunar) New Year (3-7 days)*	February 4-6
Ching Ming (Spring grave cleaning)*	April 4
Easter Holidays (4 days)	April 17-20
Tuen Ng (Dragon Boat	

Festival)*	June	5
Queen Elizabeth's Birthday	June	13
Monday following Queen's Birthday	June	15
Saturday preceding Liberation Day	August	29
Liberation Day (last Monday)	August	31
Day following Mid-Autumn Festival*	September	12
Chung Yeung (Fall grave cleaning)*	October	5
Christmas	December	25
Boxing Day	December	26

HOTELS

You have a wide choice of international-class business hotels in Hong Kong. The busiest seasons are from January to May (especially April) and from September to December (especially October), and you should book your hotel accommodation well in advance during these times. Most of the best hotels are located in the main tourist areas in Kowloon and Hong Kong island but more economical accommodation can be found in Wanchai and on upper Nathan Road. Full details of addresses and rates are available from the Hong Kong Tourist Association, which has offices in major cities around the world. A 10 percent service charge is usually added to the bill.

LOCAL TIME

Local time in Hong Kong is eight hours ahead of Greenwich Mean Time throughout the year.

MEDIA

More than 65 newspapers and 510 periodicals are published in Hong Kong. There are some 50 Chinese-language daily newspapers. The English-language newspapers are the *South China Morning Post* and *The Standard*. Local editions of the *Asian Wall Street Journal* and the *International Herald Tribune* also are printed in Hong Kong.

MEDICAL FACILITIES

Treatment at government hospitals is extremely cheap, but somewhat lacking in comfort. Hong Kong has a few private hospitals staffed by foreign and foreign-trained doctors where a visitor can receive treatment on a par with that in the West. These include Canossa Hospital and the Hong Kong Adventist Hospital. It is important to get good medical insurance as charges for private hospitals and doctors are relatively high.

NAME CARDS

It is common practice to exchange business cards when meeting individuals in Hong Kong. Cards can be ordered through most hotels and banks, and they take about two to three days to be printed. About 200 name cards should suffice.

NIGHT LIFE

Hong Kong is well-endowed with places to go at night, from well-elbowed bars frequented by buyers at the leading hotels to the girlie bars in Wanchai and Tsimshatsui. There are also numerous nightclubs (which can be very expensive), and discos. Concert and theater fare is available at the Cultural Centre, City Hall, and the Arts Centre, the main focal points of cultural activity, where good films can also be seen more often than at the local cinemas. All of these establishments are frequented by both Westerners and locals.

A form of entertainment enjoyed by the majority of Hong Kong Chinese is gambling, whether it be high-speed mahjong, horse racing or visiting the casinos in nearby Macau.

RELIGION

Most religions are represented in Hong Kong. There are over 360 Buddhist and Taoist temples and monasteries, the Anglican Cathedral of St. John's and numerous churches of nearly all Christian denominations as well as mosques, Hindu and Sikh temples and gurudwaras, and a synagogue. There are several monasteries on Lantau Island, including the Buddhist Po Lin monastery and Trappist monastery, with others at Shatin and Tsuen Wan.

TIPPING

Hong Kong does not have a general sales tax, but there is a service charge of 10 percent added to all hotel and most restaurant bills. A 5 to 10 percent tip is expected at restaurants also. Tipping is not mandatory, but it is generally expected, for taxi drivers, bell boys, doormen and toilet attendants.

A BRIEF HISTORY

With a total area of 1,070 square kilometers, Hong Kong consists of more than 200 islands and islets and a portion of the mainland, east of the Pearl River estuary, adjoining the Chinese province of Guangdong. The largest part of Hong Kong is the New Territories, north of urban Kowloon up to the Shenzhen River. Hong Kong's development into a commercial center began in the 1840s after part of the territory was ceded to Britain.

At the end of the 18th Century, British merchants, restricted to a small warehouse or 'factory' area on the Pearl River near Guangzhou (Canton), established a successful trading industry, especially in the export of tea. However, a shortage of silver bullion in India and Europe led to the use of opium as payment for goods brought into Canton. These opium transactions resulted in a net outflow of silver and strained China's resources. In 1839, the Chinese Special Commissioner enacted a law prohibiting such trade and sequestered all opium stocks. British and Chinese hostilities over this action led to the First Opium War of 1840-41. As a result, China ceded Hong Kong Island to Britain under the terms of the Treaty of Nanking (1842). Fourteen years later, renewed friction over the interpretation of trading rights led to another war. The 1885 Treaty of Tientsin ended the war and gave the British the right of diplomatic representation in China. Hostilities began again one year later, and the Convention of Peking signed in 1860 included a clause ceding to Britain the southern part of the Kowloon peninsula and Stonecutters Island. In 1898, Britain leased the New Territories from China for 99 years.

Since its founding in 1841, Hong Kong has depended on international trade for its existence. In the first 100 years it relied on entrepôt trade, moving goods between east and west, taking full advantage of its strategically located harbor at the hub of Asian trade routes. Maritime trade flourished and the territory blossomed until interrupted by World War II. Japan occupied Hong Kong from 1941 to 1945. During this period 60 percent of the population fled, mostly to mainland China. Trade was paralyzed and the economy was in a shambles. In the post-war years, Hong Kong received a huge influx of Chinese immigrants and its population swelled from 600,000 to approximately 2,400,000 by early 1950. By then, Hong Kong's economy, based solely on its role as an entrepôt, was no longer able to support its growing population. Despite a scarcity of usable land and virtually no natural resources, manufacturing began in textiles and garments led by Shanghai industrialists. Export driven growth led to the rise of modern Hong Kong as one of Asia's economic "tigers" in the 60s and 70s.

On December 19, 1984, the governments of the United Kingdom and the People's Republic of China signed the Sino-British Joint Declaration on the future of Hong Kong. The Joint Declaration states that China will resume sovereignty over Hong Kong on July 1, 1997 and that, for 50 years after that date, Hong Kong's capitalist system and lifestyle will remain unchanged.

The Joint Declaration was formally ratified by both governments on May 27, 1985, marking the beginning of the 12-year transition period to July 1, 1997 when Hong Kong will become a Special Administrative Region (SAR) of the People's Republic of China. The SAR will retain the status of a free port, of being a separate customs territory, and that of being an international financial center. Its markets of foreign exchange, gold securities and futures will continue. There will be free flow of capital after 1997 and the People's Republic of China will not levy taxes in the SAR. The policies of the People's Republic of China for the future of Hong Kong have been laid out in the Basic Law, which will in effect become Hong Kong's constitution after 1997.

The Chinese Government, which was responsible for drafting the Basic Law, appointed the Basic Law Drafting Committee, which comprised representatives from Hong Kong and China. The Committee put the finishing touches on the Law on February 17, 1990, and decided that 18 of the 60 Legislative Council (Legco) seats should be directly elected. This proportion is to rise to 40 percent in 1999 and 50 percent in 2003.

A policy of non-interference in each other's internal affairs has also been agreed upon in the Basic Law.

Although the Basic Law lays down the rules of conduct come 1997 there are potential trouble spots looming large over Hong Kong. Hong Kong has become a port of first asylum for Vietnamese refugees. Progress towards stemming the growing number of Vietnamese boat people arriving and repatriating them has been slow. Emigration continues to drain Hong Kong's work force of many of its most affluent and skilled members. The intense demonstrations held in Hong Kong against China's regime following the Tiananmen Square incident were not sustained over 1990 and 1991. But sporadic protests against the

Chinese government do occur. And with the direct election of 12 "liberals" to Legco in September 1991 it is likely that Hong Kong's journey to 1997 will continue to be eventful.

MAJOR HONG KONG GOVERNMENT CONTACTS OVERSEAS

Hong Kong Trade Development Council (HKTDC) Offices

Head Office
36th-38th Floors
Office Tower
Convention Plaza
1 Harbour Road
Hong Kong
Tel: 584-4333
Tlx: 73595 CONHK HX
Fax: 824-0249
Cable: CONOTRAD HONG KONG

EUROPE

Prinsengracht 771-773
1017 JZ Amsterdam
The Netherlands
Tel: (020) 627-7101
Tlx: 15081 HKTDC NL
Fax: 31-020-622-8529
Cable: CONOTRAD AMSTERDAM

2 Vassileos Alexandrou Street
Athens 11634
Greece
Tel: (301) 724-6723/4/5
Fax: (301) 724-8922

Balmes 184
Barcelona 08006
Spain
Tel: (3) 217-62-50
Tlx: 97862 SARP E
Fax: (3) 415-47-48
Cable: PUBLICRELATIONS
    BARCELONA 6

PO Box 500551
D-6000 Frankfurt/Main 50
Germany
Tel: (069) 586011
Fax: 069-5890752
Tlx: 414705 COFRA D
Cable: CONOTRAD FRANKFURT

Ilancilik Reklam Ajansi A.S.
Piyalepasa Bulvari
Kastel Is Merkezi
D.Blok Kat: 5
80370 Piyalepasa
Istanbul
Turkey
Tel: (901) 154-98-60 (6 lines)
Fax: (901) 154-98-67

Swire House, Ground Floor
59 Buckingham Gate
London SW1E 6AJ
England
Tel: (44) 1 828-1661
Tlx: 916923 CONLON G
Fax: (44) 1-828-9976

Cable: CONOTRAD LONDON SW1

2 Piazzetta Pattari
20122 Milan
Italy
Tel: (02) 865405
Tlx: 333508 HKTDC 1
Fax: 39-2-860304
Cable: KONGTRAD MILAN

18 rue d'Aguesseau
75008 Paris
France
Tel: (01) 47-42-41-50
Tlx: 283098 HKTDC F
Fax: 33-1-47-42-77-44

Kungsgatan 6
S-111 43 Stockholm
Sweden
Tel: (08) 100677
Tlx: 11993 TDC S
Fax: 46-8-7231630
Cable: CONOTRAD STOCKHOLM

Rotenturmstrasse 1-3/8/24
A-1010 Vienna
Austria
Tel: (0222) 5339818
Tlx: 115079 HKTDC A
Fax: 43-222-5353156
Cable: CONOTRADREP WIEN

Bellerivestrasse 3
8008 Zurich
Switzerland
Tel: (01) 3832950
Tlx: 817850 CONZ CH
Fax: 41-1-383-08-13
Cable: CONOTRAD ZURICH

NORTH AMERICA

333 N. Michigan Ave., Suite 2028
Chicago
Illinois 60601

United States
Tel: (312) 726-4515
Tlx: 728335 HONG KONG CGO
Fax: 1-312-726-2441
Cable: CONOTRAD CHICAGO

Suite 1100, National Building
347 Bay Street
Toronto
Ontario M5H 2R7
Canada
Tel: (416) 366-3594
Tlx: 06218056 HKTDC TOR
Fax: (416) 366-1569
Cable: CONOTRAD TORONTO

CENTRAL AMERICA

Apartado Postal 6-4510
El Dorado
Panamá City
Republic of Panamá
Tel: (507) 69-5894
Fax: (507) 69-6183

ASIA

Room 901, 9th Floor
CITIC Building
19 Jianguomenwai Dajie
Beijing
China
Tel: (86) 1 500-2255
Tlx: 22927 HKTDC CN
Fax: (86) 1-500-3285

20 Kallang Avenue
2nd Floor, Pico Creative Center
Singapore 1233
Tel: (65) 293-7977
Fax: (65) 292-7577

12th Floor, Quanta Place
678 Tun Hwa South Road

Taipei
Taiwan
Tel: (886) 02 705-9333
Tlx: 23288 QUANTA
Fax: 886-02-705-9222

Toho Twin Tower Building
4th Floor, 1-5-2 Yurakucho
Chiyoda-ku, Tokyo 100
Japan
Tel: (03) 3502-3251/5
Tlx: J26917 HKTDCT
Fax: (03) 3591-6484
Cable: CONNOTRADD TOKYO

AUSTRALIA

GPO Box 3877
Sydney, NSW 2001
Australia
Tel: (02) 299-8343/6
Tlx: AA121313 CONSYD
Fax: 61-2-290-1889
Cable: HONGKONREP SYDNEY

MIDDLE EAST

New Juma Al-Majid Building
Dubai Sharjah Road
Dubai
United Arab Emirates
Tel: (9714) 665-950
Tlx: 46361 MARKET EM
Fax: (9714) 667-114
Cable: MARKETS DUBAI

Visas ■ Air travel to India ■ Getting around in India ■ City travel ■ Taxis ■
Buses ■ Health precautions ■ Climate ■ Clothing ■ Accommodation ■
Business hours ■ Public holidays ■ Food and drink ■ Currency and credit
■ Numbers ■ Shopping ■ Entertainment ■ Social etiquette ■ A brief
history ■ Indian embassies

INDIA

INDIA'S GRADUAL OPENING up to business travelers and tourists has seen steady improvements in the facilities that cater for the foreign visitor — hotels, transportation and the service industries. But for the first-time visitor the encounter with India can be a traumatic one. Some familiarity with "the way things operate" and insights into the logistics involved in a business trip can lower the chaos level that is encountered. A little historical and cultural background helps make sense of things too. However, there is no escaping the psychological impact of the first visit to a society whose contradictions are plainly on view, rather than hidden away. The encounter with pollution, poverty, the sick, grossly disfigured beggars, hawkers and touts, families of street sleepers, open sewers and debris is unavoidable — if you intend to venture outside the hotel doors, particularly in the overcrowded city of Bombay.

Being prepared for these encounters is as important as getting ready for business calls, if you want to begin to feel at ease in this business environment.

VISAS

Entry visas are required of all foreigners who intend to take up residence for business or professional reasons or to take up employment or permanent residency. Visas can be obtained from Indian embassies and consulates or from British embassies in countries without an Indian representation. Applications can be processed in person or by mail.

Business and **tourist visas** are valid only for six months from the date of issue and permit a stay of three months, extendable on application for another three months.

Transit visas are valid for three months and allow for a maximum stay of 15 days only.

Direct transit visas for connecting flights are available on arrival and are valid for 72 hours.

Special permission is required (as per the stamp on your visa) to visit certain restricted areas, such as the northern districts of West Bengal.

AIR TRAVEL TO INDIA

India's four major international airports are well-served by the world's airlines with 50 international carriers operating over 175 flights a week.

The advantage of the country's geographical location is that it is well-placed for international air routes. This is only slightly offset by the fact that a large majority of flights seem to take off and land in the early hours of the morning en route to "prime time" landings in Europe, North America and Southeast Asia.

GETTING AROUND IN INDIA

Air Travel

Indian Airlines, the domestic carrier, covers one of the world's largest domestic networks. It carries over 26,000 people every day to 85 destinations including all the major business centers. Although demand for seats far outstrips supply, reservations have been greatly eased by computerization in the last few years, and a quota of seats for foreign visitors is usually available. Reservations can be made from abroad, and travelers with a busy schedule coming to India in the peak season (September - March) are advised to book early.

The airline has a fairly good safety record, although it is notorious for delays and cancellations. But the fare structure makes its flights some of the least expensive in the world.

Vayudoot, the second, considerably smaller state-run airline, can get you to a further 35 locations not catered to by Indian Airlines.

Rail

With more than 10 million passengers per day, 11,000 trains, 7,000 stations and 62,000 kilometers of track, Indian railways is the second-largest rail system in the world. Efficient and fairly reliable in terms of train schedules, its reservation queues have also been reduced by computerization in the last couple of years. More than one foreign businessman has managed to get from Bombay to Delhi within a reasonable time — when he was unable to get a seat on an airplane -- by taking an overnight express. But generally demand for seats (especially first- and second-class air-conditioned berths) is great and advance booking is important.

Road

Roads range from bad to passable by most Western standards, and the overcrowding adds to the unpleasantness of a business trip by road. However, if a long trip to a factory is required, your supplier will usually transport you in a chauffeur-driven, sturdy, white Ambassador car. Do not be fooled by appearances — even though the design of the car is 1960s-vintage — your actual vehicle may be only six months old. Your driver will be skilled at negotiating the perils of the road, including what seems like irrational and unsafe driving habits of other road users. If you are frightened by the excesses of your own driver (and this applies to taxi-drivers also) you can ask him to slow down. But you need to be aware that the norms of driving in India are very different than those you are used to, and may well continue to be so for some time. While recent legislation makes it compulsory for the rider of a motor scooter in Delhi to wear a crash helmet, only the driver will wear one. His wife sitting sidesaddle in the pillion position will not, nor will the baby in her arms, nor the 4-year-old standing in front of the driver with his hands on the handlebars.

CITY TRAVEL

Airport coaches are available at the four major airports to transport passengers to the respective city centers. Several airlines can also arrange for chauffeured cars to take you from the airport to your hotel. It is often the case that — given the innate graciousness of Indians generally — your business client/host will pick you up in his own car or arrange for you to be picked up, if he knows your flight details.

TAXIS

Metered taxis are available in every major city. The local yellow-topped, black-bodied taxis are metered but with escalating prices the meters are nearly always out of date. To help regulate fares and to prevent wholesale exploitation of passengers, cards with the latest increases are printed periodically by the government and are available in the taxi. In 1991, for instance, the charges for a taxi journey in Bombay were approximately five times the amount shown on the meter. As with taxi drivers around the world, some have a reputation for trying to make extra money. Make sure the meter flag is down before the journey has commenced, or you might end up in a long conversation about the fare at the end of the journey. Even with metered fares the occasional driver will want to tell you his hard luck story or try to cajole you into paying more than you should. Most old hands recommend maintaining a sense of humor and being willing to banter with the driver, while standing firm about paying what it really cost. As one old hand puts it:

> " You can always give him the money and walk away. They never come after you. And even if they do, a quick word with the nearby policeman or hotel doorman will soon put him in his place. After all he is just trying to cheat you. And many Indians who take pride in (and make a living out of) honoring guests, don't like that one little bit."

When in Delhi on business it is cheaper to hire a taxi for a whole day to cover the expansive city, than it is to hire taxis on a visit by visit nature.

Chauffeured, white-bodied, air-conditioned taxis are also available for hire from most hotels.

Three-wheelers (modified motor scooters) are also available in the suburbs of Bombay and in the centers of most Indian cities, but their open sides, slowness and low sitting in the road make them a poor and very dirty second choice for city travel, even at half the taxi fare.

The last resort in some cities is the pedal-tricycle, often pulled by scrawny and not-too-healthy-looking Indians. Only if you are quite light, have plenty of time, like to see people sweat or are desperate to get across town and have no other means of transport, is this slow form of human-powered travel a real option.

BUSES

Interstate luxury buses are interesting and relatively comfortable options for side trips during a business visit, but city buses like city trains tend to be incredibly overcrowded, and should be avoided. It is not uncommon in all of the major cities to see single-decker 36-seater buses housing over 100 people, including eight or nine youths clinging to the outside of the open bus door.

HEALTH PRECAUTIONS

Eradication of smallpox and the decreasing incidents of cholera have meant greatly relaxed health regulations for visitors in recent years. However, staying healthy in India does take some common sense behavior and careful planning. While inoculations are no longer required by the government for entry — with the exception of Yellow Fever certificates for those arriving from infected areas — many doctors and consulates still advise a range of protective inoculations before going to India. These include cholera and tetanus shots, and a gamma globulin shot to protect against hepatitis and anti-malaria pills. In keeping with the long-term concerns over the AIDS epidemic all business residents are required to produce an AIDS free certificate or undergo an AIDS test.

While in India the onset of "Delhi-belly" (an upset stomach) is to be expected with the change of climate, food and water. The country's summer heat is hard on even the most seasoned traveler, let alone the newcomer, while spicy food and increasing pollution in the cities add to the strain an unacclimatized businessman has to deal with. But stomach troubles are usually a temporary state lasting a couple of days, while your body adjusts to its new environment.

With careful eating habits and basic attention to sanitation any illness should be just a temporary setback, but should your condition linger, hotels can help with their own doctors or can refer you to several excellent doctors in the vicinity of your hotel. International brand name medicines are available, as is competent hospital treatment in the case of a medical emergency.

One often cited piece of advice "don't drink the water" is fairly sound — with the exception of prepared water in the hotels provided in flasks. Avoid overly spicy food for the first few days and street stall food for your entire visit if you want to be on the safe side.

CLIMATE

Although India is classified as a tropical monsoon country, it has a wide variety of climates and land types within its borders: the snow capped Himalayas; hot sandy deserts; tropical jungle; fertile alluvial plains and arid hill plateaus. Likewise its climate is equally varied with extremes of hot and cold in the north and little temperature variation in the equatorial south. West India is dry while East India is humid. A strong monsoon usually inundates Bombay and Calcutta every year while a second weaker monsoon affects some parts of southern India every winter.

The summers in Delhi can be extremely hot, while Bombay and Calcutta summers generate less heat but high humidity. The most pleasant time to visit India for business or otherwise is between November and March when the temperatures in most of the country are at a tolerable level. In Delhi and the north, winter night temperatures can drop steeply, and warm clothing is advisable.

Average minimum and maximum temperatures (in degrees Centigrade) in the main cities are:

City	Maximum	Minimum
Madras	32.7C May	24.5C Jan
Calcutta	31.1C May	20.2C Jan
Bombay	30.1C May	24.3C Jan
Delhi	34.3C June	14.3C Jan

CLOTHING

Business clothing style in India is generally quite relaxed — in marked contrast to that of the Asian NICs. In Bombay especially, business suits and ties are the exception rather than the rule, with the main business clothes for executives being an open-necked business shirt and slacks. Safari or leisure suits are worn by many businessmen. More formal attire is adopted by a few companies and for particularly important business occasions, but as a rule climate and custom dictates casual attire.

Loose-fitting and cotton clothes are advisable for the whole year, particularly during the humid days of summer, and heavy clothes and woolens are needed for the two to three months of a northern Indian winter.

ACCOMMODATION

Most businessmen, on short visits to India will stay at one of the several Indian-run four- or five-star hotels in the major cities. These hotels — set up by well-established Indian businesses — have achieved international recognition for the high quality of their services. These chains — including the Oberoi hotels, Taj (Tata Company) hotels, and Welcome group hotels run by the private sector, and the public sector Ashok Group — offer luxury accommodation and service at rates far below those of comparable high-end hotels in developed countries or in most of the Asian NICs.

Business guests working with large companies will often be housed in company guest houses, complete with a personal staff to take care of their needs. This is particularly true if the visitor needs to spend some time in on-site visits at out of the way locations.

BUSINESS HOURS

The normal work week is five and a half working days, and while hours of business vary a half to one hour between cities, they follow this general pattern:

Banks
Monday — Friday	8.45 am - 5.45 pm
Saturday	8.45 am - 2.15 pm

Commercial banking hours
Monday — Friday	11.00 am - 3.00 pm
Saturday	11.00 am - 1.00 pm

Government Offices
Monday — Friday	10.00 am - 5.00 pm
(Closed on Saturday)	

Other businesses
Monday — Friday	9.00 am - 5.00 pm
Saturday	10.00 am - 12.00 pm

PUBLIC HOLIDAYS

The number of statutory holidays vary from state to state with over 52 annual major religious and secular events to choose from. However, the holidays that affect India as a whole are usually 19, of which several are governed by the lunar calendar and are on different dates every year. The 1992 public holidays are:

Republic Day	January 26
Maha Shivratri*	March 2
Holi*	March 19
Id-ul-Fitr*	April 5
Mahavir Jayanti*	April 15
Good Friday*	April 17
Buddha Purnima*	May 16
Half-yearly closing of bank's accounts	June 30
Id-ul-Azha*	June 12
1st Muhurram*	July 11
Independence Day	August 15
Janmashtami*	August 21
Milad un-Nabi*	September 10
Gandhi Jayanti	October 2

Dussehra*	October 5
Deepavali*	October 25
Guru Nanak Jayanti*	November 10
Christmas Day	December 25
Yearly closing of bank's accounts	December 31

Dates marked with an asterisk (*) vary from one year to the next.

While being aware of these dates helps the businessman to more usefully plan his trip, the events themselves offer opportunities to participate in the local culture.

FOOD AND DRINK

Indian cuisine is famous throughout the world for its rich variety and exotic flavors. Spiced curries, seafood, tandoori meats, and a wealth of vegetarian dishes are available in hotels and high-end speciality restaurants in all the major cities. A bountiful supply of fresh fruits, nuts and vegetables is also indigenously grown. For the first-time visitor the fiery vindaloos and kheema curries should be eased into once the palate has grown accustomed to its new environs. For the over indulgent the Indian breads, cucumbers and yogurt have a way of taking the fire out of a too-hot curry. It is also wise to avoid drinking water while you negotiate the curry. It only makes the taste more fiery. A word of advice from a British consultant is to not drink while eating a hot curry but to drink two or three glasses of water on finishing it. If you look around you will notice several of the locals are following the same pattern.

Western food, Chinese, Thai and other ethnic cuisines are available in all the leading hotels, at very reasonable prices.

CURRENCY AND CREDIT

The currency of India is in decimal denominations. Until 1975 the rupee (the basic unit of currency) was pegged to the pound. Since then its value has been determined in relation to a basket of international currency units of India's major trading partners. Its value against the US dollar has steadily drifted downward in the last 14 years, dropping from US$1 = Rs8.04 in 1983 to US$1 = Rs25.75 in late 1991.

Bank notes are in units of 1, 2, 5, 10, 20, 50, 100, and 500 rupee denominations. One hundred paise are equal to one rupee. Coins are

45

in 5, 10, 20, 25 and 50 paise units as well as in 1, 2, and 5 rupee denominations.

International credit cards are accepted in most major restaurants, hotels and shops.

Converting hard currency to rupees can only be done through recognized channels in India such as hotels, banks and authorized exchange dealers. As Foreign Exchange Regulation Act (FERA) regulations don't allow rupees to be reconverted to hard currencies without proof that the rupees were legitimately acquired in India, it is important for the foreign businessman to keep currency transaction forms given to him at the time of the exchange of his currency for rupees. Equally important for visitors bringing in more than US$1,000 cash is the Currency Declaration Form completed on arrival that must be presented on departure. Failure to produce these can result in delays and awkward situations at the airport, where the outgoing traveler cannot legally change his rupees nor leave with them. Settlement of these dilemmas can end up with the businessman losing money in the ensuing negotiation to resolve the dilemma.

NUMBERS

India's unique system of counting higher amounts of money can be confusing to the newcomer. One *lakh* is equal to 100,000 and one *crore* is equal to 10,000,000. Commas are also used in a different way to denote these Indian amounts. A sum of 100,300,000 rupees is represented as 10,03,00,000 rupees (or 10 crores and 3 lakhs).

SHOPPING

India is a shopper's dream with intricate handmade goods of high quality available at extremely low costs including:

> Handwoven Persian style carpets from Kashmir
> Semiprecious and precious jewelry
> Textiles
> Carved figurines
> Marble inlay work
> Metalwork
> Leather goods

For safe shopping government emporia and shops on the approved list of the Department of Tourism are the best bet. Bazaars are also there for the visitor who wants to try his hand at bargaining, but beware the taxi driver's favorite shops. His commission is probably built into the price you are going to pay.

ENTERTAINMENT

Night life is in limited supply in India, and no all-night Western-style nightclubs and girlie bars — as per Hong Kong and Bangkok — are socially acceptable in the more traditional Indian environment. Having said that, the bigger cities do have a number of bars and discotheques — usually in hotels — that do have a moderate flavor of Western-style entertainment.

However, the local entertainment and cultural attractions are well worth taking in. Indian dance and music festivals are often put on in hotels and museums, art galleries and movies are available. English-language films are shown on video in your hotel room and at a few local cinemas. If you want to try your luck with a Hindi film (the Indian film industry is the largest and most prolific in the world), be sure to go with an Indian friend who can explain the main points of dialogue — and sit back for a three-hour, musical soap opera. Catering to the masses, these films are usually pretty simple, in the good-guys-wear-white-bad-guys-black genre, and give a flavor of what the masses in India — who don't own TVs — find entertaining.

In addition, there are the many festivals in India which a visitor can participate in, or simply observe.

SOCIAL ETIQUETTE

Some basic tips for the business visitor that will stand him in good stead with his Indian hosts are:

    1) Remove your shoes before entering temples, mosques or gurudwaras.

    2) Do not take photographs in places of worship (for religious reasons), or airports (for security reasons).

    3) For women visitors, conservative morals dictate that dresses that cover the legs and tops that cover the shoulders are more acceptable than the mini-skirts and vest tops of contemporary Western fashion. The exception to this are hotels where foreigners are the majority residents.

    4) Do not automatically shake hands with women. Tra-

ditionally women don't touch men in public, and the *namaste* (folded hands) greeting is expected. Indian businessmen, especially urbanites, on the other hand will expect to shake your hand, as an accepted opening to a business encounter, usually followed by the exchange of name cards.

5) To eat with your hand is taken as a sign of affirmation of Indian ways, and is worth a try. But always and only use your right hand.

6) Likewise, the handing over of cash is done with the right hand.

7) Feel free to indulge in conversations about politics and sports (especially cricket) — two abiding passions in a fairly free-speaking and free-thinking society.

8) Avoid religious arguments and harping on the inadequacies of the country. This will only hurt or embarrass your hosts.

9) Good humor and jokes are appreciated, as long as it is playful and does not insult your host's country. It is far safer to let him jest about what is happening in India than it is for you to do so.

10) Tipping in India is not obligatory but expected. Ten percent or less is usual for waiters, porters, bellboys, etc. It is a wise move to get a supply of small notes (Rs 5, 10, 20) at the outset of your visit, for this purpose.

A BRIEF HISTORY

Early Civilizations
The earliest civilization on the Indian subcontinent can be traced back to 2500BC — a highly developed urban culture in the Indus river valley.

By 1700BC this culture was falling into decline and Aryan migrants from Persia (now Iran) were beginning to become the dominant civilization. The Aryans established agriculture and pastoral activities. The natural fertility of the land and the prosperity generated by agriculture and cattle breeding gave plenty of leisure time to this culture, allowing a highly reflective theology and religion to develop. The basic tenets of Hinduism, the Vedas (the Hindu scriptures), the concept of the castes and the Sanskrit language all emerged during this period.

Population pressures and the rise of individual ownership saw the emergence of a society divided into rich and poor between 1000BC and

600BC. The 6th Century BC gave birth to the religions of Buddhism and Jainism, as the Buddha and Mahavira separately sought alternate answers to the contradiction of great wealth coexisting with abject poverty, than the ones provided by Hinduism.

With the growth of population putting pressure on land as property, and with the society divided into specific functions, power struggles and conflicts began to emerge. States and empires emerged as forms of organized power to put down disorders. These vast empires include the Magdha Empire (ruled by the converted Buddhist Ashoka) and the Mauryan empire.

The Gupta Age of the 4th Century AD covered much of India and for two centuries there was a resurgence of Hinduism and several advances in science and literature.

The early medieval period saw an expansion of Indian agriculture, with a growth in irrigation innovations. With only the wealthy peasant being able to afford the new water wheel, the gap between rich and poor grew. In addition, the caste tradition forbade many peasants from owning land, establishing a large pool of landless laborers — a situation that continues to this day.

The Mughal Invasions and After

A new wave of invaders from Central Asia in the 13th Century brought the stamp of Islam to India. For 320 years the Delhi Sultanate controlled the subcontinent and established a centralized bureaucracy for revenue collection and general administration. In addition the Mughals brought new innovations such as the spinning wheel, new architectural techniques, and a scientific, cultural and artistic flowering.

The Indian economy flourished with expanding trade links to the Middle East, Europe and China. The Mughal empire also saw an increasing establishment of European traders in India itself.

When the empire crumbled in the 18th Century the relative communal harmony that had existed for centuries gave way to religious clashes. The empire disintegrated into fiefdoms and princely states, and invaders from abroad sought to carve out a piece of territory for themselves. Or, like Nadir Shah from Iran, they sought merely to plunder the famous riches of India and return home.

The Marathas carved out something of an empire in the West and North of India under the leadership of the non-Brahmin Shivaji, but the power vacuum was waiting for a new imperial power. Britain was to fill it.

The Imprint of British Control 1759-1947

The British were not the first to colonize India in its 5,000-year-old history, but it was under the British that the forces that dominate modern India's economy and economic policies were given form.

The original British influence in India was established through a trading company, the East India Company. In the century up to 1859, from humble beginnings in the East, it extended British influence over most of India, through a mixture of trade, diplomacy, military actions and alliances with local rulers.

On the positive side, the British introduced many elements of industrial infrastructure that helped improve the Indian economy, such as roads, steamships, modern factories, the railway and telegraph. And hand in hand with these modern means of communication and transport came modern concepts of social organization: a civil administration, the rule of law and equality before the law, and the outlawing of social evils such as widow-burning and female infanticide.

On the negative side, the manipulation of the Indian economy to the end of serving Company and British aims led to the increased taxation of the general populace, the restricting and banning of Indian goods (like textiles, that were in direct competition to inferior British-made goods) with the subsequent impoverishment of many artisans and traders; the ongoing exploitation of Indian raw materials for British use; and the flooding of the Indian market with British-manufactured items.

Resentment reached a flash point with the Indian Mutiny of 1857 when both Hindus and Muslims fought to bring an end to British rule. After 18 months, the mutinous forces eventually lost out to the better armed and coordinated forces of the British and their Indian supporters. The British government took over direct control of British interests in India, increasing its army to prevent unrest, and playing on the potential for enmity between Muslim and Hindu to prevent any repeat of the kind of unity present during the Mutiny.

The Growth of Indian Political Power 1880-1947

The failure of the Mutiny led some Indians to see that new methods were required to successfully protest against alien rule in India, based on organized strength, and within the framework of British Law and policies. In 1885, the Indian National Congress was formed by British-trained lawyers and other highly educated Indians as a forum for political awareness and action. In 1906 the All India Muslim League, with its mandate to protect the rights of the minority Muslim community, was established. The political seeds of modern India and Pakistan were sown.

The mobilization of a mass movement of civil disobedience in the 1920s and 1930s, under the spiritual leadership of Mahatma Gandhi and the political leadership of Nehru's Congress Party, put increasing pressure on the British to "Quit India". Through the boycott of British goods, strikes, and a variety of non-violent protests, the British government and its international standing as the rightful ruler of the subcontinent received severe setbacks, while the Congress as a political movement grew from strength to strength. (Even so, from a trading perspective, it is worth noting that in 1926, India was the fifth largest exporting nation in the world.)

Independence and a New Economic Framework
India emerged on the world scene as a sovereign nation in 1947, on the tide of anti-colonialism that had been rising across the world since the early 1900s, and which, intensified by the turmoil of World War II, had become irresistible. With Britain exhausted by the War, and the British government in the hands of a Labour Party sympathetic to the calls for Indian independence, India was suddenly devolved from British control.

India's birth as an independent nation was a bloody one, with millions of migrating Hindus and Muslims running the gauntlet of sectarian violence en route to new homelands in India and Pakistan.

While other developing nations relied heavily on foreign aid and investment to build their national economies in the 1950s and 1960s, India chose to follow a different economic pathway, that of **self-reliance** and **state-controlled development**.

Rising domestic demand and intense competition in world markets restricted India's exports during 1950-70. India's share in total global exports declined from 2.1 percent in 1950 to 1.1 percent in 1960, though world exports doubled during this period.

By the mid-1960s India's heavy industries had become well-established and the "green revolution" was beginning to bring India to self sufficiency in foodgrains. The government began to recognize the importance of exports as an economic activity, and steps were taken to encourage export production. Exporting organizations, promotion councils, commodity boards and trade development bodies were set up by the government to organize and enhance export efforts. With this support, India's annual growth rate in exports increased from 4.1 percent in 1968-69 to 7 percent in 1973-74, to an average of 13 percent a year between 1983-84 and 1987-88.

Despite periodic ethnic and religious conflicts, India's democracy has proven to be a remarkably stable one, with freedom of speech and assembly, a rule of law and an independent judiciary, and relatively free and fair elections. In November 1989, a broad coalition government was elected to power on an anti-corruption ticket. The Janata Dal which came into power did not have an absolute majority. The Congress was still the largest parliamentary group. However, the

Janata Dal was supported from the outside by the Bharatiya Janata Party (BJP) and the Left Front (Communists) and thus commanded a majority in parliament.

After one and a half years in power there were serious differences between the Janata Dal and the BJP culminating in the BJP withdrawing support as a result of the Ayodhya dispute and the introduction of the Mandal commission based caste reservations announced by V.P. Singh's Janata Dal government.

A section of the Janata Dal split from the party and this faction formed a government with the support of the Congress. However this government also fell after only four months in office when the Congress party threatened to withdraw support. The then Prime Minister Chandrashekar resigned and fresh elections were declared.

The resultant 1991 election was one of the most violent since independence, marked as it was by the tragic assassination of Congress leader Rajiv Gandhi. The Congress party improved its performance but fell short of absolute majority. However, it was able to form a government by virtue of being the largest party in Parliament. The government of P.V. Narashima Rao won a vote of confidence and has since been in power. The new government has been able to introduce rapid reforms toward liberalizing the Indian economy.

INDIAN EMBASSIES

India has diplomatic representation in over 100 countries. Listed below are the representatives in major countries.

Argentina
The Embassy of India
Cordoba Avenue
950, Pisco 4
1054, Capital Federal
Buenos Aires

Australia
The High Commission of India
3-5, Moonah Place
Yarralumla
Canberra ACT 2600

Belgium
The Embassy of India
217, Chausse de Vleuragat
Avenue 1050

Brussels

Brazil
The Embassy of India
SDS Edifi Venancio VI
5th Andar
CAIXA Postal 11-1097, 70.463
Brasilia D.F.

Canada
The High Commission of India
10, Springfield Road
Ottawa KIM IC 9

Chile
The Embassy of India
871, Triana

P.O. Box No. 10433
Santiago

China
1, Ri Tan Dong Lu
Beijing

Czechoslavakia
The Embassy of India
Valdstejnska 6
Malastrana
Prague 1

Denmark
The Embassy of India
Vengehusvej 15
2100
Copenhagen

Egypt, Arab Republic of
The Embassy of India
5, Rue Aziz
Abaza Street
Zamalek
Post Box 718
Cairo

France
The Embassy of India
15, Rue Alfred Dehodencq
75016 Paris 16

Germany
The Embassy of India
262/264, Adenaueralle
5300 Bonn 1

Hong Kong
Commission of India
16/F, Block D
United Centre
95 Queensway Road
Hong Kong

Hungary
The Embassy of India
14, Buzaviragutea 1025
Budapest II

Indonesia
The Embassy of India
51, Jalan Rasuna Soud
Kuningan
Selatan
Jakarta

Italy
The Embassy of India
Via Venti Settembere, 5
Rome 00187

Japan
The Embassy of India
2-11, Kudan Minami
2, Chome
Chiyoda-Ku
Tokyo 102

Jordan
The Embassy of India
Jabal Amman, 1st Circle
Post Box 2168
Amman

Kenya
The High Commission of India
Jeevan Bharti Building
2/F, Harambee Avenue
P.O. Box No. 30074
Nairobi

Korea (South) Republic of
The Embassy of India
37-3, Hannam-dong
Youngsan-Ku
G.P.O. Box 3466
Seoul

Kuwait
The Embassy of India
34, Share Istiqlal
Bousheri Building
P.O. Box No. 1450
Safat

Malaysia
The High Commission of India

Wisma Selangor Dredging
20/F, West Block
142 C, Jalan Ampang
Kuala Lumpur 50450

Mexico
The Embassy of India
Avenida Musset 325
Colonia Polanco
1550 Mexico 5, D.F.

Netherlands, The
The Embassy of India
Buitenrustweg 2
The Hague

New Zealand
The High Commission of India
180, Molesurth Street, 10/F
Wellington

Nigeria
The High Commission of India
107, Awolowo Road
P.M.B. 2322, South West Ikoyi
Lagos

Norway
The Embassy of India
30, Niels Juels Gate
Oslo 2

Pakistan
The Embassy of India
482 F, Sector G-6/4
Islamabad

Philippines
The Embassy of India
2190, Pariaso Street
Dasmarinas Village
P.O. Box No. 926 Mcc
Makati Metro
Manila

Poland
The Embassy of India
Rejtana 15, (Flats 2-7 Mokotow)

Warsaw 02 516

Portugal
The Embassy of India
Rua das Amoreiras 72 D
6/F
1200 Lisbon 1

Saudi Arabia
The Embassy of India
Ibrahim Masoud Building
Medina Road
Baghdadia
P.O. Box No. 952
Jeddah

Singapore
The High Commission of India
India House, No. 31 Grange Road
Kiliney Road
P.O. Box No. 92
Singapore 0923

Spain
The Embassy of India
Avda de P.O. XII 30-32
Madrid 28016

Sri Lanka
The High Commission of India
State Bank of India Building
Sir Baron Jayatilake
Mawatha P.O Box 882
Colombo 1

Sweden
The Embassy of India
Adolf Fredriks Kyrkojata 12
P.O. Box 1340 S-11183

Switzerland
The Embassy of India
Weltpoststrasse 17
Berne 3015

Thailand
The Embassy of India
46, Soiprasarmitr

Sukhmiut 23
Bangkok

Turkey
The Embassy of India
Cinnah Caddessi 77 A
Cankaya
Ankara

United Arab Emirates
The Embassy of India
Plot No. C 34, Sector E 9
Adma-Opco Computer Bldg.
Khalifa Bin Zayed Street
P.O. Box 4090
Abu Dhabi

United Kingdom
The High Commission of India
India House
Aldwych
London WC2B 4NA

USA
The Embassy of India
2107, Massachussetts Ave. N.W.
Washington D.C. 20008

USSR
The Embassy of India
No. 6-8, Ulitsa Obukha
Moscow

Venezuela
The Embassy of India
Quinto Tagore, 12 Avenida
San Carlos
La Floresta
Apartado de Cerreos 61585
Caracas 106

Zimbabwe
The High Commission of India
12, Natal Road
Belgravia
P.O. Box No. 4620
Harare

C H A P T E R

KOREA

4

Passports and visas ■ Air travel to Korea ■ Getting around Korea ■ Getting around Seoul ■ Trains ■ Accommodation ■ Air raid drill ■ Business attire ■ Business hours ■ Communications ■ Currency ■ Entertainment, eating out and night life ■ Electricity ■ Geography and climate ■ Language and people ■ Local time ■ Medical care ■ Name cards ■ Newspapers ■ Radio and television ■ Public holidays ■ Shopping ■ Silence routine ■ Tipping ■ Travelers checks and credit cards ■ A brief history ■ Diplomatic missions abroad

KOREA

ON THE FACE of it, Korea is much like any other modern country, particularly in Seoul, which has seen rapid development in recent years to the point where it is hardly distinguishable in its essentials from any other sophisticated capital. Behind that face, however, lie some unique characteristics, destined to catch unaware visitors off their guard. True, Korea treads some basic Asian paths, but it goes its own way in some traditional areas. It pays to know about them for your own comfort and that of your hosts.

PASSPORTS AND VISAS

Most nationalities visiting Korea are granted admission for at least 15 days without having to obtain a visa. However, holders of the following passports are permitted to stay without having to obtain a visa for the following periods of time:

Up to three months: Austria, Bangladesh, Belgium, Britain, Chile, Columbia, Costa Rica, Denmark, Dominican Republic, Germany, Finland, Greece, Holland, Iceland, Liberia, Liechtenstein, Luxembourg, Malaysia, Mexico (except diplomatic and official visits), Norway, Pakistan, Peru, Singapore, Spain, Surinam, Sweden, Switzerland, and Thailand.
Up to two months: Italy, Lesotho, Portugal, and Turkey.
Up to one month: France and Tunisia.

Applications for a visa can be made to any Korean Embassy abroad. Once in Korea, if you need to stay longer than you had anticipated, then you must go to the District Immigration Office at least 14 days before the expiration of your existing visa and apply to obtain an extension of stay to your visa. The telephone numbers of these offices are:

Seoul (02) 776-8984
Kimpo Airport (02) 662-7611
Pusan (051) 463-7161
Kimhae Airport (051) 98-1871
Cheju Airport (064) 22-3494

AIR TRAVEL TO KOREA

Korea has three international airports — Seoul's Kimpo Airport (the most commonly used), Kimhae near Pusan, and Cheju on Cheju Island. A new international airport is planned to be built in Chongju by 1993.

Seoul is a regular destination for most major airlines flying out of Europe, North America, North Africa, the Middle East, and other parts of Asia. Some flights are direct — British Airways, for example, operates a weekly non-stop flight between London and Seoul. Others connect through places such as Hong Kong or Japan.

In the new Korea World Trade Center, a City Air Terminal is now operating for businessmen flying into and out of Seoul. This service not only provides speedy immigration processing to avoid long queues at the airport, but it also takes businessmen straight to where much of Korean business operates under one roof.

There is an airport tax of 6,000 won when departing.

GETTING AROUND KOREA

By air — Korean Air Lines operates domestic services between Seoul, Pusan, Taegu, and Cheju Island. For details and reservations, telephone Seoul (02) 756-2000. However, because distances are short, flights take an average of only an hour and the road and rail networks offer good viable alternatives.

By rail — The Korean National Railroad has a reliable and extensive railway network connecting major centers such as Seoul, Pusan, Mokpo, Kwangju and Kyongju.

By sea — There are frequent hydrofoil services to the ports and the outlying islands of Korea. For further details, telephone Seoul (02) 752-4644.

There are also ferry services operating from Pusan to Japan. One service operates daily (except Saturday) to Shimoneseki. For further details, telephone Seoul 738 0055 or Pusan 463 3165. The other service goes twice weekly to Osaka. For further details, telephone Seoul 754-7784 or Pusan 463-7000.

GETTING AROUND SEOUL

Taxis — Taxis are abundant, but during rush hours or inclement weather the demand is high and they are difficult to find. There are two types of taxis available. Small Pony cabs charge lower rates than the larger "88" taxis (Daewoo, Royale, and Hyundai Stellar). Regular small car taxi fares are 700 won for the first two kilometers and an additional 50 won for every 353 meters thereafter. The larger "88" taxis have fares of 800 won for the first two kilometers and 100 won for every 483 meters thereafter.

It should be noted that it is common practice for taxi drivers to demand a flat fee of several thousand won during busy traffic periods and inclement weather if your destination is more than 800 meters or to the city suburbs. This is illegal, but a common practice.

Rides are generally inexpensive compared to most Western countries — to travel from one end of the center of Seoul to the other, the fare should be roughly 1,300 won. It is advisable to have your destination written down in Korean even though taxi drivers were allegedly all taught to speak basic English before the country hosted the Olympics in 1988. Call taxis, ordered by telephone, have a starting rate of 1,000 won. The telephone number in Seoul is 414 0150-9.

To take any taxi after midnight, a 20 percent surcharge is added, but they are not easy to find in any case at that time of the night.

Buses — The city bus system is complicated, with all operations in Korean. Once the numbers of various bus lines have been learned by the foreign visitor, they offer cheap and convenient transportation. In addition to the regular buses on which most passengers stand, there are "sit-down" buses. Sit-down buses have fewer stops and are air conditioned. Fares are 150 won for regular buses and 400 won for sit-down buses. They are not recommended for anyone but the adventurous with time to spare. However, there are airport buses that run from Kimpo Airport to all the major hotels in Seoul. These services run every ten minutes and operate between 5.30 am and 9.30 pm — the fare costs 500 won one way. There is also an efficient inter-city bus service.

Subway — Seoul has one of the most attractive subways in the world. The system is modern, rapid, clean and inexpensive, with four lines going to two zones. The cost of fares ranges between 200 and 400 won.

TRAINS

Korean National Railroads maintains an extensive network of railways which connects far-flung points throughout the peninsula with Seoul and other major cities. Korea's first railway service was inaugurated in September 1899, and prior to the Korean War, one could travel from Pusan to Paris by train! The country's railway network suffered serious damage during the Korean war, but since 1953, railway lines have been expanded and modernized.

There are five types of railway services. Foreigners usually opt for the fast *Saemaul* super-express trains with air-conditioning (or heating) and dining cars.

Seats may be reserved and tickets purchased up to 10 days in advance of scheduled departures. Reservation and advance ticket sales may be arranged at railway stations or through local travel and tourist agencies.

The Korean National Railroad's main office is located at the following address:

> *Korean National Railroad*
> *168, 2-ga, Bongraedong*
> *Chung-ku*
> *Seoul*
> *Tel: 392-7811*

ACCOMMODATION

International class hotels have mushroomed in Seoul and Pusan over the past few years, particularly to cater to the 1988 Olympics and the many conferences that are attracted to Seoul. There are also motels and *yogwans*. *Yogwans* are traditional simple Korean-style hotels, often providing floor mattresses, known as a *yo*, and public bathing. However, these facilities are gradually being modernized and the average cost per night in a *yogwan* is US$20. Almost all major hotels have swimming pools, night clubs, shopping arcades, and telex and secretarial services. Advance reservation is recommended during the peak tourist seasons in the spring and fall.

The best known first-class hotels are the Hilton, Chosun, Hyatt, Regency, Lotte, Plaza, Seoul Garden, Sheraton Walker Hill and Shilla, costing approximately US$80-150 a night plus a 10 percent service charge. The average amount charged for a room in the more standard hotels is about US$55 per night.

AIR RAID DRILL

An official peace treaty between South and North Korea has never been signed, and as a result, military activity is rife, spreading its tentacles into everyday life. Be prepared for air raid drills. If one occurs while you are on the street, you will be required (along with everyone) else to go to the nearest shelter — for about half an hour. You will be ushered along with the crowds.

BUSINESS ATTIRE

Most Korean businessmen and women dress smartly — men usually wear dark suits — and visitors are expected to do the same. Short-sleeved shirts are acceptable in the summer. Foreign businesswomen are advised to wear conservative attire. The Korean custom of removing shoes at the door is sometimes applied to factories as well as offices, in which case there are slippers kept by the door. A visitor is sometimes given the choice.

BUSINESS HOURS

Regular business hours are from 9 am to 6 pm Monday to Friday, and 9 am to 1 pm on a Saturday. Banks are open between 9.30 am and 5 pm and 9.30 am to 1.30 pm on Saturdays. A lunch "hour" in a Korean businessman's day tends to start at midday and extends to about 2.00 pm.

COMMUNICATIONS

Korea is a modern country with up-to-date telecommunication and postal facilities. All incoming and outgoing mail in Korea is subject to government inspection. International telephone calls can be made directly through international subscriber dialing (ISD) or with operator assistance. Phonecards for ISD can be purchased at hotels, airports, and post offices and used in the gray-colored magnetic card-reading phone booths. All first-class hotels offer ISD on room phones but a heavy surcharge is added. For operator-assisted calls, dial either 1035 or 1037 in Seoul, and 117 in other areas. For further information, dial 1030 in Seoul.

Fax and telex are widely used throughout Korea.

CURRENCY

The local currency is the won. There are no restrictions on how much money can be brought into Korea but any amount over US$10,000 or equivalent must be declared on arrival on the Foreign Exchange Record. There are notes for 1,000, 5,000, 10,000 won and coins for 1, 5, 10, 50, 100, 500 won. In the main shopping areas, US dollars are readily accepted.

Banking hours in Korea are 9.30 am to 5.00 pm on weekdays and 9.30 am to 1.30 pm on Saturdays.

ENTERTAINMENT, EATING OUT AND NIGHT LIFE

Koreans like to greet the evening with a few drinks among friends. Liquor of any sort is nearly always taken together with *anju* (snacks), which can range from peanuts and dried seaweed to a dazzling range of hot and cold dishes.

One of the traditional dishes served with many Korean meals is *kimchi*. There are many different types — some stronger than others — but basically it is a mixture of pickled cabbage or cucumber with chile and garlic, traditionally made by fermenting it over the winter in jars buried in the ground. Garlic, raw and cooked, is consumed in great quantities.

Rice wine is a common accompaniment to meals. There are two types, *sake* and *soju*. A liquid is available in most restaurants which can be added to the wine to reduce the effect of the alcohol if desired.

ELECTRICITY

The voltage is being gradually changed from 100 to 220. Hotels usually provide outlets for both, but it is wise to check the sockets before using any electrical appliance you have brought along with you.

GEOGRAPHY AND CLIMATE

The Republic of Korea covers the Southern half of a peninsula which juts out from the northeastern edge of Asia. It occupies an area of

99,000 square kilometers, roughly equal to the size of Iceland or Portugal. In terms of topography, low hills in the south and west gradually change to higher mountains toward the east coast and the north. Most of the major rivers drain from the western and southern sides of the peninsula into the Yellow Sea and the South Sea. With only 20 percent of the land arable, agriculture is intensive.

While the country's eastern coastline is relatively straight, Korea's western and southern coasts are irregular with many inlets, small peninsulas and bays. Most of the country's 3,000 islands located off the western and southern coasts are rocky and uninhabited.

Korea has four distinct seasons and a climate similar to that of the eastern United States. Typically, the long and pleasant springs are followed by hot and humid summers with monsoon rains. Autumn is crisp and cool while winters tend to be extremely severe, often with biting winds, and temperatures can plummet to -15 Centigrade or below. Almost 70 percent of the annual precipitation of 75 to 100 centimeters of rainfall is recorded between June and September.

LANGUAGE AND PEOPLE

With over 42 million people, Korea is one of the most densely populated countries in the world. Roughly 20 percent of the work force live in rural areas and are engaged in agriculture and fishery, although cities attract an increasing number as the country continues to industrialize. Concentration of the population is greatest in the capital city, Seoul, with about 11 million people, followed by Pusan with some four million. The growth rate in the urban population has averaged 5 percent in recent years.

The Korean language and way of life grew from the ancient Altaic culture which once thrived from the Russian Urals all the way across central Asia to Siberia, long before the time of Confucius. Korea was the easternmost point of the Altaic culture, which has put a permanent stamp on Korean life. Even today, the Korean language resembles Finnish and Turkish more than it does Chinese or Japanese. The alphabet, Hangul, consists of uniquely Korean characters. Many Koreans speak English, but Westerners frequently find the accent difficult to comprehend.

This Altaic heritage has been the underlying cohesive force binding Koreans together through the millennia of its turbulent history and foreign intrusion. However, in outward appearance and behavior, Koreans today reflect the Japanese, Chinese, and Western influences which have molded their recent history. Unlike the Chinese, however,

Koreans maintain strict public decorum and reverent formality among themselves. Yet unlike the sometimes rigid Japanese, Koreans are very warm, emotional and quick to laugh. In Korean culture, poise and passion balance like the *yin* and the *yang*, and each has its own place and time.

LOCAL TIME

Korean Standard Time is nine hours ahead of Greenwich Mean Time except during British Summer Time when it is 10 hours ahead.

MEDICAL CARE

The international hotels have good medical facilities. Drugs and other medicines are obtained from pharmacists; many have familiar trademarks but are made locally under joint ventures. Translating the prescriptions, however, may prove difficult. Pharmacies in Korea are well stocked with modern medicines and are carefully monitored by government authorities.

No vaccinations are required to enter Korea from another country. However cholera, yellow fever, and hepatitis injections are recommended for those arriving from infected areas.

It is not advisable to drink water straight from the faucet or even from flasks provided in hotels.

NAME CARDS

Name cards are freely exchanged at first meetings. It is amazing how many can be got through in a short period, so err on the generous side when having yours printed. Two hundred would not be too many for an extended trip of two or three weeks.

NEWSPAPERS

Six nationally distributed papers are currently published in Korea, including one in Chinese and two in English. They appear daily except for Mondays (newspaper staff do not work on Sundays) and major national holidays. The two English language newspapers are *The Korea Herald* and *The Korea Times*.

RADIO AND TELEVISION

Four major Korean radio stations broadcast throughout the country. In addition, American Forces Korea Network (AFKN) operates eight transmitters which broadcast programs 24 hours a day across the country (except Cheju island). AFKN programs are entirely in English. There are two Korean television broadcasting networks with affiliates throughout the country. They are the Korean Broadcasting Service (KBS-TV) and the Munhwa Broadcasting Company (MBC-TV).

PUBLIC HOLIDAYS

New Year holiday	January 1-3
Folk Customs Day (lunar calendar)	January 1
Independence Movement Day	March 1
Arbor Day	April 5
Buddha's Birthday (lunar calendar)	April 8
Children's Day	May 5
Memorial Day	June 6
Constitution Day	July 17
Liberation Day	August 15
Choosuk (Full Moon Festival) (lunar calendar)	August 15
Armed Forces Day	October 1
National Foundation Day	October 3
Hangu (Korean Alphabet) Day	October 9
Christmas Day	December 25

SHOPPING

Seoul has many shopping areas: arcades — many of them underground — department stores, and markets. Major department stores are open from 10.30 am to 7.30 pm seven days a week, but the smaller shops tend to open early and stay open until late. Prices are fixed in the majority of stores, but bargaining is possible in the markets. The cheapest and most famous area for shopping in Seoul is Itaewon, but look out for counterfeit goods. Everyday domestic items can be purchased from department stores, the arcades and the supermarkets.

SILENCE ROUTINE

A practice which can catch you unawares is the "six o'clock silence", although it is possible to go to Korea many times and not come across it. Where it is practiced, it happens when the national anthem is broadcast at 6.00 pm on the radio. A foreign businessman may suddenly find himself talking into thin air while his counterparts stand in silent respect until the anthem is finished.

TIPPING

Tipping is not generally expected in Korea. A 10 percent service charge is added to all hotel bills and most restaurant bills. Taxi drivers don't require tips, unless they perform a special service, such as carrying your bags, but small change is appreciated. In addition, a cash tip would not go amiss in drinking salons and similar establishments that provide a hostess service. Unless specifically prohibited, bellhops generally receive 150 won per bag.

TRAVELERS CHECKS AND CREDIT CARDS

Money is easily exchanged in foreign exchange banks and all major hotels readily accept US dollars or travelers checks. Major credit cards are widely accepted.

A BRIEF HISTORY

The beginning of Korean history is often dated to 2333BC when Tan-gun, a legendary figure born of the son of a god and a woman from a bear-totem tribe, established the first kingdom named Choson (or the "land of the morning calm"). While the authenticity of the Tan-gun myth is disputed, it is known that ancient Korea was characterized by clan communities which combined to form small city-states. Their prominence rose and fell until by the First Century BC, three king-doms — Koguryo (37BC to 688AD), Paekche (18BC to 660AD), and Shilla (57BC to 935AD) — emerged on the peninsula.

Ever since Shilla unified the peninsula in 668AD, Korea has been ruled by a single government and has maintained political independence and cultural and ethnic identity in spite of frequent foreign invasions. Foreign intrusions were attempted by the Khitans, Mongols, Manchus, and the Japanese.

Korea became the focus of intense imperialist competition among China, Russia, and Japan in the late 19th Century. In 1910, Japan annexed Korea and instituted a brutal colonial rule. This stimulated the growth of nationalism among the Koreans. Korean intellectuals were infuriated by Japan's repressive official assimilation policy. They asserted their differences and struggled to distance themselves culturally from their colonial masters.

By the 1930s, Korea was the industrial base for Japan's war efforts in China. When it was liberated in 1945, there were some hydroelectric plants and chemical industries (mostly in northern Korea) which had rich natural resources, as well as a network of railways and telecommunications.

The Founding of the Republic

As a result of the polarization of post-war global politics, Koreans faced the division of their country. Before the end of the war, the allies at Yalta had secretly decided that Korea, like Germany, would become a trustee of the allied victors. In accordance with this exclusive pact, the United States and the Soviet Union occupied Korea after the war and brought with them the Cold War rivalry, which later divided the peninsula.

Korea underwent confusion as right and left wings confronted each other, and nationalist leaders, who had returned after having taken part in the overseas campaigns of the colonial period started competing against one another for political leadership. In 1948, general elections were held in the southern half of the peninsula to found the Republic of Korea, and Syngman Rhee was appointed as President.

Most Koreans were enraged with the division of their country and this led to the tragic Korean War (1950-53). The entire land was devastated and millions of people were left homeless and separated from their families. A cease-fire was signed in July 1953, and both sides have since gone through enormous changes in their efforts at rehabilitation.

Reunification remains a sacrosanct issue for people on both sides of the vigilantly guarded Military Demarcation Line. Nevertheless, despite the thawing in Korea's relationship with the Soviet Union, 40,000 U.S. troops remain stationed in South Korea. In addition, deep ideological differences among Koreans themselves conspire to keep the fortified boundary as seemingly impenetrable as ever.

DIPLOMATIC MISSIONS ABROAD

Argentina
Coronel Diaz 2860
Buenos Aires
Argentina
Tel: 83-2736, 83-5498, 84-8865
84-9964

Australia
113 Empire Circuit, Yarralumla
Canberra, A.C.T. 2600, Australia
Tel: 733044, 733956, 733586

Austria
Reisnerstrasse 48
1030 Vienna
Austria
Tel: 725811/2

Bahrain
P.O.B. 5564, 941/6 Gooful
Manama
The State of Bahrain
Tel: 252161, 233825, 261710

Brazil
SEN-Avenida das Nacoes Lote 14
70436 Brasilia
D.F., Brazil
Tel: 225-2567, 4202, 3303
Myanmar
591 Prome Road Kamayut
Yangon, Myanmar
Tel: 30497, 30655

Cameroon
B.P. 301, Yaounde
Cameroon
Tel: 22-3223, 22-1725

Belgium
Avenue Hamoir 3, 1180 Brussells
Belgium
Tel: 375-3980

Bolivia
Avendia 6 de Agosto

2592 La Paz
Bolivia
Tel: 364485, 364512

Canada
151 Slater Street, Suite 608
Ottawa, Ontario KIP 5H3
Canada
Tel: 232-1715/7

Chile
El Vergel
2422 Santiago
Chile
Tel: 23-7742

Denmark
Dronningens Tvaergade 8
Kobenhavn K, Denmark
Tel: (01) 143123, 144705, 147907

Finland
Annankatu 16 B 50, 00120
Helsinki 12, Finland
Tel: 642509, 642500

France
125 Rue De Grenelle
75007 Paris, France
Tel: 705-6410

Germany
53 Bonn, Adenauerallee 124
Germany
Tel: 218095/6

Greece
105-107 Vassilissis Sofias Avenue
Athens, Greece
Tel: 644-3219, 644-3210

Guatemala
16 Calle 3-38 Zona 10
Guatemala
Tel: 680302

India
9 Chandra Gupta Marg
Chanakyapuri Extension
New Delhi-110021, India
Tel: 690303

Indonesia
JL. Gatot Subroto, Jakarta
Selatan, Indonesia
Tel: 512309, 516234

Italy
Via Barnaba Oriani
3000197 Rome, Italy
Tel: 805306, 805292, 878626

Ivory Coast
01, B.P 3950 Abidjan 01
3ème étage, Immeuble
"Le Generale" Avenue du Général de
Galle, Abidjan
Cote-d'Ivoire
Tel: 22-5014, 32-2290

Japan
2-5, Minami-Azabu, 1-Chome
Minato-Ku, Tokyo, Japan
Tel: (03) 452-7611/9

Jordan
Jabal Amman 3rd. Circle Abu
Tamman Str., Amman, Jordan
Tel: 42268

Kenya
6th Floor, Kencom House
Government Road, Nairobi, Kenya
Tel: 28011, 29012, 332839

Kuwait
Damascus Street, Block 12
Division 42, House No. 12
Kuwait
Tel: 513242, 531816
554206, 554235

Malaysia
422, Jalan Pekeliling

Kuala Lumpur, Malaysia
Tel: 482177, 482234, 482314

Mexico
Av. Homero 823, Col. Polanco
Mexico 5, D.F. Mexico
Tel: 254-1499, 254-1916

Netherlands
Koninginnegratcht 25
The Hague
Netherlands
Tel: 070-469634

New Zealand
Williams City Centre, Plimmer
Steps, Wellington, New Zealand
Tel: 739-073/4

Norway
Bjorn Farmannsgt. 1, Skillebekk
Oslo 2, Norway
Tel: 562211/2

Philippines
Room 201-208, Rufino Building
123 Ayala Avenue
Makati, Metro Manila
Philippines
Tel: 886423, 886897, 887712,
886813, 886417, 886859, 8180046

Portugal
Edificio Aviz, Bloco 3-13
Rua Latino Coelho 1
1000 Lisbon, Portugal
Tel: 533505, 535943

Saudi Arabia
P.O. Box 4322, Mohammed
Hamza Fatayerji Bldg, Al-Musa
Adiya, Jeddah, Saudi Arabia
Tel: 55073, 55074, 55061

Singapore
Room 2408-2414, 24/Fl Shaw Centre
Scotts Road
Singapore 0922

Tel: 7376411, 7376334, 7376098
   7376782

Spain
Avenida de Generalisimo
Madrid 16
Spain
Tel: 2628504/6, 2624560

Sri Lanka
No 98, Dharampala Mawatha
Colombo 7
Sr Lanka
Tel: 91325, 95084

Switzerland
Kalcheggweg 38, 3006 Berne
Switzerland
Tel: (031) 431081/2

Taiwan
345, Chung Hsiao East Road
Section 4, Taipei 105, Taiwan
Tel: 761-9363

Thailand
6th Floor, Pra-Parwit Bldg
28/1 Surasak Road, Off Silom
Bangkok, Thailand
Tel: 234-0723/6

Turkey
Cinnah Caddesi Ala, Can Sokak
No. 9 Cankaya, Ankara, Turkey
Tel: 262590, 264858, 262589
   270074

United Arab Emirates
Khamis Al Rumaithi Villa
Plot 164, Sector Wlo/22
Karama St. Abu Dhabi
United Arab Emirates
Tel: 337635, 338337

United Kingdom
4, Palace Gate, London W8 5NF
United Kingdom
Tel: (01) 581-0247/9, 0250

United States of America
2320 Massachusetts Avenue
N.W., Washington, D.C. 20008
U.S.A.
Tel: (202) 483-7383

Venezuela
Ota. Algeria, Av. El Paseo Con La
Calle
Occidente, Qta. Alegria Prado Del
Este, Apartado No. 80671, Caracas
1080, Venezuela
Tel: 77-0556, 77-3433, 978-1357

C H A P T E R

MALAYSIA

MALAYSIA

AFTER THE "1990 Visit Malaysia Year" the major cities and resorts in the country have all been spruced up with lights, festivities and friendly smiles. Accommodations are of good quality in the country and you can basically expect pleasant service in hotels. No longer do tourists visit Thailand and Singapore and bypass Malaysia, as the country has in recent years become a recognized destination for tourists and business travelers alike. Moreover, Malaysia's well-organized information and efficient transport system make it easy to get around the country.

PASSPORTS AND VISAS

Most visitors with an internationally recognized travel document do not require a visa when visiting Malaysia.

Commonwealth citizens (excluding those from India), British Protected Persons and citizens from Ireland, Switzerland, the Netherlands, San Marino and Liechtenstein do not require visas for entry into Malaysia. For visits up to three months other than for employment, visas are not required by citizens of Austria, Belgium, Denmark, Finland, France, Japan, Germany, Iceland, Italy, Luxembourg, Norway, Sweden, South Korea, Tunisia and the United States.

Visa requirements are waived for visitors from ASEAN countries such as Indonesia, the Philippines, Thailand, Brunei and Singapore who intend to stay in Malaysia for up to one month. Taiwan citizens must apply for a special document issued by Malaysian missions abroad. Citizens of all other countries do not need visas for a 14-day stay, except for nationals of Albania, Bulgaria, China, Czechoslovakia, Hungary, Israel, Cambodia, Laos, Mongolia, North Korea, Poland, Romania, South Africa, Taiwan, the USSR, Vietnam, Yugoslavia and Zimbabwe. Nationals of Bulgaria, Czechoslovakia, Hungary, Romania, Yugoslavia, Poland and the USSR are, however, allowed a stay of one week without a visa.

To enter Sabah and/or Sarawak, visitors need additional permission from the immigration departments of the respective states.

Visitors intending to stay for longer periods should apply for a visa before going to Malaysia. Visitors who are granted visas or permits to reside in Malaysia for more than one year are required to obtain a National Registration Identity Card. For more information, contact the nearest Malaysian commissions or embassies.

TRANSPORTATION

Air: Many international airlines fly to Kuala Lumpur and some also call at Penang and Kota Kinabalu. The city center is half-an-hour's drive from Kuala Lumpur's Subang International Airport. Local destinations can be reached by the Malaysian Airline System (MAS), which operates numerous domestic services to destinations throughout Malaysia.

Malaysian Airlines System
Bangunan MAS
Jalan Sultan Ismail
Kuala Lumpur
Tel: 03-261-0555
Tel: 03-774-7000

Subang Information Center
Kuala Lumpur
Tel: 03-776-1014

BUSES

Internal transport is relatively efficient and cheap. Scheduled services of coaches -- most of them air-conditioned -- link all the major towns in Peninsula Malaysia. The main bus station in Kuala Lumpur is at Pudu Raya Terminal. Buses to east coast states can be taken at Putra Bus Station. Air conditioned express buses from Kuala Lumpur to Singapore cost M$17, to Butterworth about M$15.50 and to Kota Bahru, M$25.

There are local shuttle service and mini buses in Kuala Lumpur. Mini buses charge a standard rate of 50 cents regardless of where you go.

TAXIS

Generally taxi drivers understand English, and it is advisable to ensure that the fare meter is activated. Long distance taxis run between all major towns, and they are often hired on a time basis. City taxis are abundant and comparatively cheap, and it costs about M$16 to travel between Kuala Lumpur and the airport, a distance of 24 km.

Taxis are usually metered in Peninsula Malaysia but not in Sabah and Sarawak. Non-air-conditioned taxis charge M$0.70 for the first kilometer and M$0.30 for every kilometer and 8 minutes of waiting thereafter. Air-conditioned taxis charge M$1 for the first kilometer and M$0.30 for each subsequent 0.8 km and 8 minutes of waiting. An additional 50 percent surcharge is added to these rates between 12 a.m. and 6 a.m. An additional M$0.10 is charged for each passenger in excess of two, and another M$0.10 per piece of luggage applicable for the entire journey.

CAR RENTAL

Most car rental agencies have offices in leading hotels, and renting a car can provide you the flexibility while minimizing the time involved in arranging for public transportation. Malaysia has 25,000 kilometers of good roads, and it is fairly easy to drive in Malaysia. Driving is on the left side of the road, following the British fashion. You need an international driving license to drive, and all drivers and their front seat passengers are required by law to wear safety belts. Rental cars are available on an unlimited mileage basis and vary between M$110 per day for economy cars to M$300 per day for luxury cars. The following are a few hire and drive car agencies in Kuala Lumpur.

Avis Rent-A-Car, 40 Jalan Sultan Ismail.
Tel: 03-2423500

Budget Rent-A-Car, 163 Jalan Ampang.
Tel: 03-2611122

Hertz Rent-A-Car, 2nd Floor, Kompleks Antarabangsa.
Tel: 03-2433433

National Car Rental, 70 Jalan Ampang.
Tel: 03-2480522

Sintat Rent-A-Car, Holiday Inn on the Park
Tel: 03-24823888

SMAS Rent-A-Car, 1st Floor, UBN Tower
Tel: 03-2307788

Toyota Rent-A-Car, Lot 5 Federal Hotel
Tel: 03-2438142

TRAINS

Malayan Railways or Keretapi Tanah Melayu provides regular service to all states in Malaysia as well as Singapore and Thailand. Schedules and fares can be obtained at the nearest tourist office or:

Kuala Lumpur Railway Station
Jalan Hishamuddin
Tel: 03-274 7424
Reservations North, Tel: 03-274 7442
Reservations South, Tel: 03-274 7443

AIRPORT TAX

Payable prior to embarkation, the airport tax varies according to the destination: M$3 for flights within Malaysia, M$5 for flights to Singapore and M$15 for flights to overseas countries.

CURRENCY

The Malaysian ringgit (dollar) is issued in notes of denominations of M$1,000, M$500, M$100, M$50, M$20, M$10, M$5 and M$1. There are coins of M$1 and 50, 20, 10, 5, and 1 sen (cents). The value of the ringgit is determined in relation to the U.S. dollar on the foreign exchange market (US$1.00:M$2.70), but the government may intervene to ensure the relative stability of the ringgit.

BUSINESS HOURS

Local time in Malaysia is eight hours ahead of Greenwich Mean Time and 13 hours ahead of U.S. Eastern Standard Time.

In some predominantly Muslim states, for example, Johor, Kedah, Kelantan, Perlis and Trengganu, Thursday is taken as a half-day and Friday as a full-day holiday in the place of Saturday and Sunday. With these exceptions, the following hours of business are observed throughout most of Malaysia:

Government office hours:

Mondays to Thursdays   8.00 a.m. - 12.45 p.m.

		2.00 p.m. - 4.15 p.m.
Fridays		8.00 a.m. - 12.15 p.m.
		2.45 p.m. - 4.15 p.m.
Saturdays		8.00 a.m. - 12.45 p.m.

Banks:

Mondays to Fridays	10.00 a.m. - 3.00 p.m.
Saturdays	9.30 a.m. - 11.30 p.m.

Business:

Mondays to Fridays	8/8:30 am - 4:15/4:30 pm
Saturdays	8/8:30 am - 12:30/12:45 pm
Shops:	8:30 am to 4:30 pm

Government offices open from 8:00 am - 12.45 pm and 2.00 pm - 4.15 pm from Saturdays to Wednesdays, from 8:00 am to 12.45 pm on Thursdays and close on Fridays in the states of Johore, Kedah, Perlis, Kelantan and Terengganu.

ACCOMODATION

Accommodation ranges from that of a moderate standard with rates from M$50 to M$80 per person per night, to first-class hotels where single room rates start around M$130 per night. Hotels in Malaysia meet international standards, but have a touch of local flavor. The Shangri-la Hotel in Kuala Lumpur is a first class hotel situated in the center of the financial district and shopping centers, and prices range from M$260 for a single room to $3,000 for a suite. Others, located on the main hotel stride of Jalan Sultan Ismail, include the Equatorial Hotel with room rates starting at M$120, the Hilton Hotel at M$140, Kuala Lumpur Hilton at M$190, Merlin Hotel from M$120 and Regent of Kuala Lumpur from M$160. Other executive class hotels include Ming Court with room rates from M$180 at Jalan Ampang and Pan Pacific Hotel with rates starting from M$260.

Most Malaysian towns have low-cost, Chinese-type hotel accommodations, commonly known as *rumah tumpangan*. Malaysia also has an extensive network of government rest houses, and bookings should be made through the Tourist Development Corporation in Kuala Lumpur. A 5 percent government tax is payable on hotel accommodation, and many hotels levy a 10 percent service charge. Tipping is not necessary unless service is particularly good.

For more information contact:

Tourist Development Corporation Malaysia
24-27 Floor, Menara Dato' Onn
Putra World Trade Centre
Jalan Tun Ismail, 50480 Kuala Lumpur
Tel: 03-2935188
Fax: 03-2935884

Malaysia Tourist Information Complex
109 Jalan Ampang
50450 Kuala Lumpur
Tel: 03-2434929

Kuala Lumpur Tourist Information Centre
Jalan Parlimen, 50380 Kuala Lumpur
Tel: 03-2936665
Tourist Information Centre
Keretapi Tanah Melayu (KTM)
Jalan Sultan Hishamuddin
50050 Kuala Lumpur
Tel: 03-2746063

EATING OUT

Eating is a national pastime. Malaysia is a paradise for food lovers with an endless variety of exotic cuisine, which mixes Chinese, Indian, Nyonya Baba and Malay delicacies. There are also authentic cuisines of each of these cultures in addition to European and Japanese food. The last two are usually served at larger hotels. Food in Malaysia is delicious and cheap, and some of the older establishments are renowned for their first-class steaks.

An interesting way of sampling local specialities is to eat at the open-air food stalls in the night markets, or at the hawker centers in shopping centers where a variety of local specialties such as *satay* (skewered meat served with a peanut sauce), *laksa* (noodles in spicy soup), *char kuay teow* (Chinese flat noodles fried with shrimps and chili), *sambal* dishes (in spicy chili sauce), and *rendangs* (meat dishes cooked with dried coconut and other spices). *Nasi lemak* -- rice cooked in coconut milk served with sambal, peanuts, spicy meat and a hard boiled egg -- is another popular dish.

Seafood is the basis of most of the Malay cuisine. Chicken and beef are also widely used. Vegetable dishes include *rojak* (Malay salad in tasty peanut and shrimp sauce), *gado-gado* (Indonesian vegetable dish with peanut sauce) and *kangkung belacan* (a local green vegetable cooked in spicy chili and shrimp paste sauce).

Nyonya cuisines, a must try in Malaysia, blend Malay and Chinese foods and originate from Melaka. Famous dishes include *kari kapitan* (chicken curry with ginger, lemon juice and coconut milk), *kerabu* (salad of chicken, and other spices) and *inche kabin* (deep fried marinated chicken served with tasty hot sauce).

Indian food is also popular in Malaysia and includes *tandoori chicken*, *roti canai* (crispy layered bread) and *biryani* (rice dishes).

Local deserts come in a variety of tasty cakes or *kuih* made from coconut, rice flour and *gula melaka* (aromated brown sugar).

CUSTOMS AND CULTURES

While customs vary with the different races, there are many that apply to all locals. For example, before entering a Malaysian home, it is polite to remove your shoes even if you are told that it is unnecessary to do so. Gestures are also different in Malaysia. It is insulting to beckon someone with one finger or with the palm up. The palms of the hands should be turned down and fingers waved toward the palm.

When accepting something from someone, it is polite to stoop a little and accept with both hands. If one hand is to be used, use the right hand, since it is not customary to take things or eat with your left hand. The left hand is usually used for personal hygiene.

Malaysians may smile and giggle more than seems usual to foreigners, but that is to hide emotions such as shyness, embarrassment, sadness and "loss of face". Public demonstrations of affection such as holding hands, kissing and touching are considered bad manners.

Invitations are sometimes extended for politeness' sake as a social gesture. To make sure if the invitation is genuine, do not accept readily, but say something like, "Thank you, but I do not want to inconvenience you." If the host insists and the invitation is sincere, it is considered impolite not to accept.

Although foreigners are excused from observing local customs, those who do will earn the respect of their Malaysian friends and business associates.

DRESS

Light clothing is advised as Malaysia is close to the equator and the climate is hot and humid throughout the year. Average temperature ranges from 32 degrees Celsius in the afternoon to 22 degrees Celsius in the evening. Clothing in the country reflects the cultural plurality. While Western clothing is popular, you will see the Malays dressed in *baju kurong*, a long flowing outfit with long sleeves (the dress is conservative but the colors of the material are often vibrant) or *baju kebaya*, a figure hugging blouse and a sarong. Indian women often wear *saris* and Chinese *cheongsams* and *sam foos* are also worn. Unless you want to attract unnecessary attention, ladies should avoid revealing outfits such as short shorts, halter tops, sleeveless T shirts, and men should not go shirtless unless they are on the beach. When invited to a wedding it is best not to wear black, white or navy-blue solid colors as they are colors for mourning. At a royal function avoid wearing yellow, which is a color associated with Malay royalty.

PUBLIC HOLIDAYS

Malaysia observes all the important festivals and celebrations of its three major races, which often follow their own lunar calendars, as well as some Western holidays among others.

Awal Ramadan is the beginning of Ramadan, the ninth month in the Islamic lunar calendar. Every day of the month, Muslims are supposed to abstain from all food and drink from the first light of dawn to sunset. People not physically up to the fast are excused, but even they can be subject to legal penalties if caught eating outside, in public during the day.

Throughout Ramadan, including on the last evening, special prayers called *Terawih* are said in the mosques at night. Out in the streets, night life becomes more lively, as people enjoy the hours in which they are allowed to eat and drink.

Hari Raya Puasa, an understandably major holiday, celebrates the end of the fasting month. *Hari Raya Puasa* falls on the first day of Syawal, the tenth month of the Muslim calendar. Celebrations usually go on for a week, although officially it is only a two-day holiday. Domestic flights are usually booked solid as families go visit their relatives in other states. During important festivals, the usually bustling city of Kuala Lumpur looks deserted.

Another important celebration is Chinese New Year. To welcome the new year, Chinese families make preparations to clean their homes, hang red banners, pay all debts and appease their gods with offerings. Reunion dinner on New Year's Eve is an important family event. Hawker stores and some retail shops, which are predominantly Chinese, usually close for the full 15 days. Many also visit their relatives in the outer states.

The Indian Deepavali, or the Festival of Lights, falls in the Tamil month of "Aippasi," to celebrate the triumph of light over darkness, and good over evil. Indian ladies dress in new and colorful saris to welcome the occasion and prayers are offered at the temple.

In all these festivals, relatives and friends of different races visit one another where guests find abundance of cakes and food to choose from. It is a Malaysian practice to have "open houses" during these celebrations, where well-wishers can drop in at all hours of the day. In open houses, all are welcome including neighbors and even friends of friends.

The Chinese will give out *ang pows* or red packets with money to unmarried guests, and some Malays have adopted the customs of offering gifts and money to children.

Each state in Malaysia has its own set of holidays, which include birthdays of sultans and other religious celebrations. The main holidays in Malaysia are as follows, although there are a number of others which apply specifically to certain states. Where holidays fall on weekends, the following working day will be observed as a holiday. Holidays marked with an asterisk (*) are observed according to the Islamic lunar calendar. Since the lunar year is about 11 days shorter than the Western year, Islamic holidays can be expected to fall about 11 days earlier in 1993, and 11 days earlier than that in 1994.

National public holidays 1992

Chinese New Year	February 4 & 5
Hari Raya Puasa*	April 4 & 5
Labor Day	May 1
Wesak Day	May 17
The King's Birthday	June 6
Hari Raya Haji*	June 11
Awal Muharram (Maal Hijrah)*	July 2
National Day	August 31
Birthday of Prophet Muhammad*	September 9
Deepavali	
(Except Sabah, Sarawak &	
Labuan)	October 26
Christmas	December 25

State public holidays

New Year's Day	
(except Johor, Kedah, Kelantan,	
Perlis Terengganu and Melaka)	January 1

Kedah Sultan's Birthday	January 20
Hari Hol Sultan Ismail	
(Johor only)	January 21
Thaipusam	
(Negeri Sembilan, Perak,	
Penang and Selangor only)	January 30
Israk & Mikraj*	
(Kedah & Negeri Sembilan only)	January 31
Federal Territory Day	
(Federal territories of Kuala	
Lumpur & Labuan)	February 1
1st Day of Ramadan*	
(Johor only)	March 5
Selangor Sultan's Birthday	March 8
Terengganu Sultan's	
Installation Day	March 21
Good Friday	
(Sabah & Sarawak only)	March 29
Nuzul Quran*	
(Kelantan, Melaka, Perak,	
Pahang, Perlis, Selangor and	
Terengganu)	March 31
Johor Sultan's Birthday	
(Johor only)	April 8
Declaration of Melaka (Malacca)	
as a Historical City (Melaka only)	April 15
Perak Sultan's Birthday	
(Perak only)	April 19
Terengganu Sultan's Birthday	
(Terengganu only)	April 29
Pahang Hol Day (Pahang only)	May 7
(Kedah, Kelantan, Perlis and	
Terengganu only)	May 20-21
Harvest Festival	
(Federal Territory of Labuan	
& Sabah only)	May 30 & 31
Dayak Day (Gawai Festival)	
(Sarawak only)	June 1 & 2
Hari Raya Haji Kedua*	
Awal Muharram*	July 2 (all states)
Birthday of Yang Dipertua Negeri	
Pulau Pinang (Penang only)	July 16
Yang DiPertuan Besar of	
Negeri Sembilan Birthday	

(Negeri Sembilan only)	July 19
Birthday of Sultan of Kelantan	
(Kelantan only)	July 30 & 31
Raja of Perlis' Birthday	
(Perlis only)	August 12
Governor of Malacca's Birthday	
(Melaka only)	August 15
Governor of Sarawak's Birthday	
(Sarawak only)	September 16
Governor of Sabah's Birthday	
(Sabah only)	September 16
Pahang's Sultan Birthday	
(Pahang only)	October 24

HISTORY

The history of the Malay Peninsula is one of migration and colonization, which have resulted in the present multitude of spoken languages, multiethnic population and the observance of various customs and traditions.

The Deutero-Malays, who are believed to be the ancestors of today's Malays, were the first immigrants. They migrated from the Yunnan province of South China around 300BC. Hindu influence in the Malay language came in the 1st century BC when Indian traders discovered the Malay Peninsula and used it as a trade stop-over between China and India.

Civilization and feudal kingdoms flourished from 600 AD. The first was developed in Langkasuka near Kedah. The Malay states were later captured by the Sumatra-based, Buddhist-Malay empire of Sri Vijaya, which established a separate kingdom at Temasik in Singapore. Soon after the Hindu empire of Majapahit with its capital in Java took over the Malay Peninsula.

Meanwhile Malacca flourished as an international trading port where merchants from China, India, Siam, Java and Sumatra traded. Islamic influence spread to the Malay Peninsula in the 12th century when Muslim traders from India and North Sumatra migrated to Malacca. Gradually the influence of Hinduism and Sanskrit on Malay culture and language was supplanted by Islam and Arabic. Literacy developed as the Muslims in Malacca adapted the Arabic alphabet to write the Malay language. The adapted Arabic alphabet, called *Jawi* is still used, although Malay is now much more commonly written in the Latin alphabet like English.

Malacca's strategic location and popularity as a port attracted the attention of the West, starting from the age of exploration. Europeans were seeking to establish their spice routes and strengthen their trading posts. The Portuguese captured the port in 1511, and their rule lasted for 130 years until the Dutch took over in 1641, and stayed for 150 years.

Events in Europe, in particular during the French occupation in Netherlands, influenced control over the Malay Peninsula. In the early 1800s, the English occupied Malacca, and two other ports: Sir Francis Light founded Penang and Sir Stamford Raffles, Singapore for the East India Company. By the 1920s, through treaties, negotiations and relentless persuasion, the three ports known as the Straits Settlements and the entire Malay Peninsula came under British protection.

Economic development flourished and large numbers of Chinese and Indians migrated to the Malay Peninsula under British colonial rule. Money-making industries such as tin mining and rubber planting attracted large numbers of Chinese to mine for tin in the mid-1800s and a flow of Indian migrants around 1910 to work in the rubber plantations. Most early migrants came with the intention of returning to their homeland after they had earned a sum of money, and therefore, policies of integration were non-existent and migrants were allowed to keep to their own community and pursue their line of occupation.

However the deteriorating political conditions in China and poverty in India prompted many of these immigrants to stay behind. Moreover, many became prosperous, and as time passed their loyalties to their homelands diminished.

The Indians and Chinese were urbanized compared to the Malays, and as a result were more influenced by the British culture and language through Christian missionary schools. Although some aristocratic Malays were schooled in the British system, many Muslims were suspicious of sending their children to Christian schools and continued their traditional activities in fishing and agriculture. As few Malays received the education necessary to participate in trade and commerce, the division of races along vocational lines became more pronounced.

The end of World War II brought on a rise in nationalism. The Alliance political party was formed to represent the interests of various racial groups and hence the original UMNO, MCA and MIC. This eventually led to *Merdeka* or Independence for the Federation of Malaya in August 31, 1957. In 1963 Malaysia was formed with the participation of Sabah, Sarawak and Singapore. Singapore, whose population is predominantly Chinese, left the federation in 1965 to become an independent republic because of irreconcilable racial differences.

Malaysia today belongs to the Commonwealth and is a strong member of the Association of South East Asian Nations, whose other members are Indonesia, Thailand, the Philippines, Singapore and Brunei. The objectives of ASEAN since its formation in 1967 have been to foster economic and political stability in the region and serve as a forum for the resolution of intra-regional differences. With a total land area of more than 3 million square kilometers and a population of more than 300 million, ASEAN produces 95 percent of the world's output in abaca, 85 percent of the natural rubber, and 83 percent of the palm oil. With substantial sources of food and energy, ASEAN has lately become a major manufacturer of textiles, light consumer products, electronics and petroleum products.

PEOPLE

Malaysia is unique in that its political culture, social and economic relationships, and communal and religious identity are expressed largely in terms or race and religion. Race and religion are intertwined, and racial-religious differences can affect the business environment. Without falling into the trap of generalizations the following are a few common traits of the different major ethnic groups in Malaysia.

Bumiputras comprise Malays, which is the predominant group, the *Orang Asli* and other indigenous peoples such as the ethnic groups of Kadazan and Iban found in Sabah and Sarawak. The Malays numerically and politically dominate Malaysia, and they are required by law to embrace the Islamic religion although there are non-Malay Muslims too, including some who embrace the religion. The Malaysian Constitution guaranties freedom of worship, and other religions in Malaysia include Buddhism, Taoism, Confucianism, ancestor worship, Christianity and Hinduism.

The *bumiputras* tend to be employed in the public service sector, but since the New Economic Policy was proclaimed in the early 1970s, many have also joined the private sector. With them, the personal touch is important and they usually like the indirect approach with the aim of building up confidence and trust. Their relaxed and open attitude should not be construed as naive. Negotiations can begin with chit-chat and personal conversation, which might seem to be a waste of time but are, in fact, ways for both sides to get acquainted and size each other up. Aggressive negotiating can easily be counterproductive. The Malays' decisions often depend on the buyer's attitude and personality, and once they feel that a bond of trust has been established, an oral agreement is often sufficient.

Although the Chinese make up a fairly large minority -- about 30 percent of the total population -- they are often divided in politics, religion and language. Many speak English, but belong to distinct dialect groups such as Hokkien, Cantonese, Mandarin or Hakka.

The Chinese are mostly seen in the private commercial sector. They are easily contacted, and most are efficient and fast in decision making. Brevity and clarity are essential when dealing with them. Keeping "face" and establishing *guan xi* (business/personal relationships) are important. Most Chinese prefer business deals which show immediate benefits rather than long-term ones.

The Indians are generally underrepresented in business, and tend to concentrate in the textile and retailing sectors. Most educated Indians are professionals, and many can be found in the area of law and medicine. With them too, personal relationships are important and their preference for low profile negotiations does not imply lack of interest.

LANGUAGE

Although *Bahasa Malaysia* or Malay is the national language, English is the *lingua franca* in business and social dealings. At one stage before the implementation of Malaysianization in the early 1980s and the increased and compulsory use of *Bahasa Malaysia*, the country had one of the highest standards of English in Southeast Asia. Today recognizing the importance of English in international trade, the government has made efforts to improve the educational standards and to promote wider use of the language. The standard of English has dropped in recent years, especially among the younger generation who are schooled in the national language, but English is still widely spoken in Malaysia, both for business and social purposes.

In fact, you will have fewer problems communicating in English in Malaysia than, say, in the British colony, Hong Kong. While Hong Kong has a large indigenous Chinese population that speaks Cantonese, Malaysia's multiethnic population uses English as the common language of communication. This is not because Malaysians do not know their national language as an ethnic Malay flight attendant in Malaysian Airline System explained to a foreigner:

 My natural tendency to speak English to a Chinese Malaysian is simply because it is much easier to communicate. It is not because she does not know Bahasa, but since Malay is my mother tongue and not hers, it makes better sense to speak English."

Although most Malaysians speak English fluently, some foreigners may not understand the Malaysian accent and slang. For example, Malaysians often refer to a stamp as a "chop" or use the word "shift" to mean "to move" or "relocate". They like to end their sentences with "lah," which is a Malay ending to soften sentences much like the Japanese "neh" or the Canadian "eh." Many also tend to use Malay substitutes for English words. This is not done intentionally, but it usually happens when they feel more relaxed in conversation.

Interpreters are not necessary for English-speaking buyers. Although most government forms are in Malay, they usually have another set in English for foreigners.

BUSINESS CARDS AND NAME TITLES

It is customary to present your business card upon meeting as a way of introduction, and it may be easier for a Malaysian to picture your name after seeing it spelt. You will notice that Malaysians usually offer their card with their right hand, and sometimes with the right supported with the left hand to be especially polite. In general avoid handing things to people or taking them from people with the left hand.

At social meetings and even while reading local newspapers and publications, you will notice that Malaysians have a complex system of titles. The most common is *Datuk* or *Dato'*. These are titles bestowed by the King of Malaysia or the *Yang DiPertuan Agung* (the Paramount Ruler) or a state ruler (Sultan). Wives of a *Datuk* or *Dato'* are known as *Datin*.

Tan Sri is a title of chivalry given by the *Yang DiPertuan Agung*. Their wives would be known as *Puan Sri*. Malay sultans are addressed as *Tuanku* and their children and grandchildren as *Tengku* or *Tunku*. The highest title of honor is *Tun* and his wife goes by *Toh Puan*. If the wife is bestowed any of the titles, however, the husband receives no title. Malaysians take these titles seriously and it is usually polite, unless they insist that you don't, to address them by their titles.

GETTING IT DOWN IN WRITING

Many successful Malaysian businesspeople have done business by way of verbal agreements with minimal legal and contractual hassles. "Paper contracts are for Europeans" is the attitude of some Malaysians, especially the older generation. A foreigner who is used to outlining details of the negotiation on paper would seem to the Malaysians to lack trust in their business relationship. Lynn Whitman, author of *Malaysia — A Foreigner's Guide* suggests:

> A better approach for the foreigner is to write up his or her own understanding of the negotiations and to ask the Malaysian colleague to endorse it. In this way the foreigner's need to have everything on paper is met, while the Malaysian's honor is not offended."

Written contracts can be politely insisted upon, and Malaysians will usually comply. Despite their aversion to paper contracts, they understand that written contracts protect the interest of both the buyer and seller. It is advisable on international trade negotiations to add an arbitration clause as a standard item of business.

A British colony until its independence in 1957, Malaysia has styled its business law, which is precise but tedious, after that of the British. Before a business contract can be finalized, a great deal of paper work including form filling, written work and amendments are required.

BUSINESS STYLE

Malaysians are easy going and make good hosts. Their approach is usually relaxed and informal. Politeness, however, is very important in all social and business interactions. When you visit a business contact in the office, the Malaysian will offer you tea or coffee, and it is polite to accept and take a few sips when invited to drink (be warned that Malaysians drink their coffee very sweet).

Although politeness is required, Malaysians take it as a display of arrogance if you are too business-like and formal. Having a good sense of humor is essential in Malaysia and foreigners are expected to blend in. A British chief executive officer of a large trading company says:

> There is only a small expatriate community here (unlike Hong Kong), and the old pompous colonial British don't exist here anymore."

To present a professional image, stick to the business attire you would adopt in most Asian cities. Foreigners should avoid looking like tourists. A shirt and tie is appropriate for business meetings, and during factory visits or less formal functions, a batik shirt will suffice. On formal occasions a light-weight jacket and tie is most suitable.

Time and venue tend to be flexible for Malaysians and negotiations can easily take place in an office, restaurant, home or even the golf course. A top manager of Sumitomo Corporation says:

> " I play golf four to five times a week, and it is all work. My clients like golf, and I get more business done in the golf course than anywhere else."

Malaysia is not a country for weight watchers, but a paradise for those who like food. Eating is a national pastime, and it is not unusual for your Malaysian host to take you to several restaurants in a day. It is polite to try the dishes offered to you. This is hardly a problem unless it is durian (a local favorite but strong smelling fruit). Food is usually delicious but could be a little spicy for some Western tastes. Malaysia offers a wide variety of rich cuisines ranging from local Malay, Chinese, Indian and Nyonya Baba specialties to Western, Japanese, Korean and gourmet food.

Once a Malaysian businessman introduced his foreign friend to his business associates at a dinner meeting. The foreigner was well received for the simple fact that he liked every dish he ate, and even asked for seconds. A long-time British expatriate says:

> " After an eight course Chinese dinner, it is not uncommon to have your Malaysian host insist that you accompany him for supper."

It is worth while remembering that dietary habits differ from one Malaysian ethnic-religious group to another. Malaysians are sensitive to the differences and usually make allowances accordingly.

Malays, who are Muslims, do not eat pork, and meat in general must be *halal* (i.e., from animals butchered in the Islamic manner — slitting the throat and draining the blood). Malays can generally eat any vegetable dish and seafood, so long as they do not fear that lard was used in the cooking.

Islam also forbids intoxicants. Although this ban is observed less universally than the prohibition on pork, even Malays who are not very religious will be reluctant to drink in public.

The Chinese eat practically everything, but some Hindus in the Indian community are strict vegetarians.

In practice, generally Malays readily eat in Chinese restaurants, simply avoiding the pork dishes, so these dietary differences should not be overdramatized. Besides, as is the case everywhere, some Malaysians are stricter and more religious than others. Still, being sensitive to cultural issues is always an asset in an ethnically diverse place like Malaysia.

Malaysians like the personal touch in business. They much prefer a personal meeting over a phone discussion, even if the issue is a simple one. A foreign buyer should avoid being pushy and aggressive. As negotiations could sometimes get sidetracked over so much ease and informality, it is important to be patient and probe carefully the issues at hand. A successful negotiator, therefore, is one who can keep the dialogue going on a business as well as personal level.

It is important for Malaysians to develop a bond of mutual trust and respect. While written contracts and documents are essential in international trade, mutual trust and understanding provide flexibility in business transactions and are key factors in a productive, long-term business relationship.

MALAYSIAN DIPLOMATIC MISSIONS ABROAD

Australia
High Commission of Malaysia
7, Perth Avenue
Yarralumla
Canberra
A.C.T. 2600
Australia
Tel: (062) 731543, 731544, 731545
Cable: MALAWAKIL CANBERRA

Austria
Embassy of Malaysia
Prinz Eugen Strasse 18
A-1040 Vienna
Austria
Tel: 65 11 42, 65 15 69, 65 63 23
Cable: MALAWAKIL VIENNA
Telex: 133830 MALAYA

Belgium
Embassy of Malaysia
414A, Avenue de Tervueran
1150 Brussels
Belgium
Tel: 762 6767, 763 0624, 763 0640, 763 0656
Cable: MALAWAKIL BRUSSELS
Telex: 26396 MALAY B

Brazil
Embassy of Malaysia
SHIS, QI.5 Chacara 62, Lago-Sul

Brasilia, D.F. Brazil
Tel: (061) 248-5008, 248-6215
Cable: MALAWAKIL BRASILIA
Telex: 613666 EBMA BR

Canada
High Commission of Malaysia
60, Boteler Street
Ottawa, Ontario KIN 8Y7
Canada
Tel: (613) 237-5182/3/4/6
Cable: MALAWAKIL OTTAWA
Telex: 053-3520 WAKOTT

Egypt
Embassy of Malaysia
7, Sharie Wadi El Nil
Madinet El Mohandessine, Agouza
Cairo, Egypt
Tel: 3460988, 3460958, 3460982
(Direct)
Cable: MALAWAKIL CAIRO
Telex: 21376 MALCA U

Federal Republic of Germany
Embassy of Malaysia
Mittel Str. 43, 5300 Bonn 2
Federal Republic of Germany
Tel: (0228)3768 03-06
Cable: MALAWAKIL BAD
GORESBERG
Telex: 885683 MALAY D

France
Embassy of Malaysia
2, Bis Rue Benouville
75116 Paris, France
Tel: 4553-1185
Cable: MALAWAKIL PARIS
Telex: MALWAKI 610848 F

Hong Kong
High Commission of Malaysia
24th Floor, Malaysia Building
50, Gloucester Road, Wanchai
Hong Kong
Tel: 527-0921
Cable: MALAWAKIL HONG KONG
Telex: 65067 MIDAH HX

India
High Commission of Malaysia
50-M Satya Marg, Chanakyapuri
New Delhi, 110021, India
Tel: 601291/2/6/7
Cable: MALAWAKIL NEW DELHI
Telex: 31 65096 WKILIN

Indonesia
Embassy of Malaysia
17, Jalan Imam Bonjol
10310 Jakarta Pusat, Indonesia
Tel: 336438, 332864, 323750, 332
864 (after office hours)
Telex: 44445 MALAY JKT

Italy
Embassy of Malaysia
Via Nomentana, 297, Rome, Italy
Tel: (06) 855764, 857026
Cable: MALAWAKIL ROME
Telex: 611035 MAKIL I

Japan
Embassy of Malaysia
20-16, Nanpeidai-machi, Shibuya-ku
Tokyo 150, Japan
Tel: (03) 770-9331/5
Cable: MALAWAKIL TOKYO
Telex: 24221 MALWAKIL J

Korea
Embassy of Malaysia
4-1, Hannam-dong, Yongsan-ku,
Seoul 140, Korea
Tel: 795-3032, 795-9203,
794-0349, 794-7205
Telex: 27382 MAWAKIL K

Netherlands
Embassy of Malaysia
Rustenburgweg 2, 2517 KE
The Hague
Netherlands
Tel: 070-506506 (3 lines)
Telex: 33024 MALAY NL

New Zealand
High Commission of Malaysia
10, Washington Avenue
Brooklyn
P.O. Box 9422
Wellington
New Zealand
Tel: 852439/852019
Cable: MALAWAKIL WELLINGTON

Pakistan
Embassy of Malaysia
224, Nazimuddin Road, F-7/4
Islamabad, Pakistan
Tel: 820147, 820148, 823140
Cable: MALAWAKIL ISLAMABAD
Telex: 54065 WAKIL PK

People's Republic of China
Embassy of Malaysia
13, Dongzhimenwai Dajie
San Li Tun, Beijing
People's Republic of China
Tel: 522-531/3
Cable: MALAWAKIL PEKING
Telex: 22122 MAPEK C

Philippines
Embassy of Malaysia
107, Tordesillas Street

Salcedo Village
Makati, Metro-Manila
Philippines
Tel: 817-45-81/85
Cable: MALAWAKIL MANILA
Telex: 64874 WAKMAN PN

Poland
Embassy of Malaysia
ul. Gruzinska 3
03-902 Warsaw, Poland
Tel: 17-44-13, 17-31-44
Cable: MALAWAKIL
WARSAWTelex: 815368

Saudi Arabia
Kedutaan Besar Malaysia di Riyadh
Kingdom of Saudi Arabia
C11, Main Road
Diplomatic Quarters
P.O. Box 94335, Riyadh 11693
Tel: 4887098, 4887100
Telex: 406822 MALWKL SJ

Singapore
High Commission of Malaysia
301, Jervois Road
Singapore 1024
Tel: 2350111
Cable: MALAWAKIL SINGAPURA
Telex: SURJAYA RS 21406

Spain
Embajada De Malasia
Paseo de la Castellana 91-50
Centro 23
28046, Madrid
España
Tel: (91) 455-0684, 455-0737
Cable: MALAWAKIL MADRID
Telex: 42108 WAKIL E

Sri Lanka
High Commission of Malaysia
87, Horton Place, Colombo 7
Socialist Democratic Sri Lanka
Tel: 94837/696591
Cable: MALAWAKIL COLOMBO

Telex: 21181 CE

Sweden
Embassy of Malaysia
P.O. Box 26053, Engelbrektsgatan 5
Tel: 08-14 59 90 (3 lines)
Cable: MWAKIL STOCKHOLM
Telex: 13416 MWAKIL S

Switzerland
Embassy of Malaysia
Laupenstrasse 37,
3008 Berne, Switzerland
Tel: (031) 25 21 05, 25 21 06
Cable: MALAWAKIL BERNE
Telex: 912458 MALA CH

Thailand
Embassy of Malaysia
35, South Sathorn Road
Bangkok 10500
Thailand
Tel: 286-1390-2, 286-7769,
286-1190/3825
Cable: MALAWAKIL BANGKOK
Telex: 87321 MALAWAKIL TH

Turkey
Embassy of Malaysia
Koroglu Sokak No: 6
06700 Gaziosmanpasa
Ankara, Turkey
Tel: (90/4) 136 12 70, 136 12 71
Cable: MALAWAKIL ANKARA
Telex: 43616 MAL-TR

United Arab Emirates
Embassy of Malaysia
Block 'B', 17th Floor (Penthouse)
Ahmad Khalifah Al Suweidi Building
Zayed The Second Street
P.O. Box 3887
Abu Dhabi, United Arab Emirates
Tel: 338112, 328262
Cable: MALAWAKIL ABU DHABI
Telex: 22630 MALWKL EM

United Kingdom

High Commission of Malaysia
45, Belgrave Square
London SW1X 8QT
United Kingdom
Tel: 01-235 8033
10041 Stockholm, Sweden
Cable: MALAWAKIL LONDON
Telex: 262 550 WAKLON G

USA

Embassy of Malaysia
2401, Massachusetts Avenue, N.W.
Washington D.C. 20008
USA
Tel: (202) 328-7700, 328-2770
Cable: MALAWAKIL WASHINGTON
Telex: 440119 MAEM UI

C H A P T E R 6

THE PHILIPPINES

GAWA SA PILIPINAS

MADE IN THE PHILIPPINES

Visas ■ Getting around in Manila ■ Health regulations ■ Currency and credit ■ Climate ■ Clothing ■ Language ■ Accommodation ■ Business hours ■ Holidays ■ Name cards ■ Communications ■ Media ■ Food ■ Tipping ■ Shopping ■ Entertainment ■ Utilities ■ Medical facilities ■ A brief history ■ Overseas contacts — Philippine trade offices

THE PHILIPPINES

THE REVIVAL OF the Philippine economy has been accompanied by the return of foreign capital, manufacturers, buyers and tourists. A businessman traveling to Manila for the first time will find getting to the Philippines the least of his problems. It is well serviced by several of the world's major airlines. However, the confusion and complexity that confronts the uninitiated buyer on arrival in the country can be daunting. This can be considerably lessened if the buyer has some basic information about doing business in the Philippines.

VISAS

Foreigners may enter the Philippines without a visa for up to 21 days if they have onward or return tickets. A temporary visit visa allows foreigners to stay for 59 days but prohibits them from undertaking employment. This period is extendible for varying periods up to a total of one year. Any foreigner who stays beyond 59 days must register with the **Commission of Immigration and Deportation**, or if he is outside Manila, with the **Office of the City or Municipal Treasurer**.

A foreigner may come in on pre-arranged employment or for the purpose of developing and directing the operations of an enterprise in which he has invested. A minimum investment of US$75,000 qualifies a foreigner for a special investor's resident visa (SIRV), which allows him, his spouse, and his children below the age of 21 to reside in the Philippines while his investment subsists.

Please note that the Philippines has reciprocal visa policies and these vary according to which country is concerned. It is advised to check visa regulations with the local Philippine consulate in your country.

GETTING AROUND IN MANILA

You can get around by hire car, taxi, bus, or "jeepneys" which are similar to minibuses. Shorter routes are served by tricycles.

For those used to the compact and efficient environments of Hong Kong and Singapore, Metro Manila can be a commuter's or a driver's nightmare. It is a sprawling metropolis of 630 square kilometers, comprising four cities, including Manila and Quezon City, and 13 municipalities. Infrastructure is fast giving way to the pressures of a rising urban population (at latest unofficial count: over eight million), and has aggravated traffic conditions. At non-peak hours, the drive from the Ninoy Aquino International Airport to Makati takes only 10 minutes. At rush hours, it can take as long as an hour.

Hire cars with drivers can be arranged at the hotels and are the most comfortable way to get to your destination. Self-drive hire cars should not be tried by first-time visitors. Sticking to one's lane is unheard of in Manila's streets and is only one of the many rules of the road that are constantly being breached by local drivers. It is said by many scarred veterans that if you can drive unscathed in Manila, you can drive anywhere else in the world.

A word of caution about taxis: insist on using the meter instead of negotiating a pre-arranged fare. Air-conditioned taxis charge P3.50 (US$0.13 at P27:US$1) for the first 500 meters and P12.50 is added at the end of the trip. For non-airconditioned taxis, the rates are P2.50 (US$0.09) and P1.00 (US$0.03) for the first 500 meters and P7.50 is added at the end of the trip. The approximate fare from the international airport to Makati in a non-airconditioned cab is P30 (US$1.11). For other destinations, inquire from the hotel desk. Street-wise commuters recommend Golden and EMP taxis for their reliable meters.

Buses and jeepneys are the cheapest ways to get around. Fares start at P1.50 (US$0.05) for the first five kilometers and 25 centavos (US$0.01) for every kilometer thereafter. But unless you have some knowledge of the city, or a companion who knows the city fairly well, it is not advisable for you to use this form of transport.

HEALTH REGULATIONS

If you are staying in Manila for the duration of your visit, vaccinations are unnecessary. However, if you're going outside Manila, you need to check the health profile of the places you're visiting and take the necessary precautions. Malaria is known to be endemic in some provinces in the Philippines.

CURRENCY AND CREDIT

The official currency is the Philippine peso which is divided into 100 centavos. Coins come in denominations of P2, P1, 50 centavos, 25 centavos, 10 centavos, 5 centavos and 1 centavo. Notes are in denominations of P100, P50, P20, P10, P5, and P2. The exchange rate fluctuates from day to day and at the time of going to press was about P27 to US$1. Check with your hotel or local banks for official rates.

Foreign currency can be changed at commercial banks and authorized foreign exchange dealers at the airport, tourist district, hotels, and big department stores such as Shoemart. There is no limit on the amount of foreign exchange that visitors can bring in, but amounts exceeding US$3,000 must be declared at all points of entry.

Major credit cards such as Visa, American Express, Diners Club, Master Card and JCB are accepted in many commercial establishments in Manila, and hotels in cities outside Manila.

CLIMATE

The Philippines has two seasons: wet and dry. In the northern part of the country, including Manila, the wet summer months are from June to October. This is the time when typhoons hit the country and flooding occurs in parts of Metro Manila due to the heavy rains. Businessmen who visit the country around this time must take into account possible traffic snarls in the busiest sections of the metropolis, including Makati, the business district. Expect late arrivals or no-shows if you have any appointments. The dry summer months are from November to May when temperatures can go as high as 33 degrees Celsius (91 degrees Fahrenheit). November to February is cool and dry. In the south, the range of temperatures is fairly similar to that in the north but rainfall is distributed throughout the year. Average annual rainfall in the Philippines is 305 cm.

The mountain regions in the north including Baguio City are cool throughout the year, and can be very cold from November to February. Baguio is four to five hours' drive from Manila.

CLOTHING

Light clothing is comfortable and appropriate during the hot and humid months. Business attire for men consists of a cotton shirt with a tie, or the native barong Tagalog, the national dress. The barong Tagalog is a light shirt worn outside the pants. Its long-sleeved dressy version is made of jusi (woven banana fiber) or pina (woven pineapple fiber) and can be worn to formal occasions. More casual versions in cotton and other light natural fabrics are suitable for office wear. Foreigners who find it difficult to dispense with the business suit for meetings with guests and associates make it a habit to bring a jacket to the office. For women, a dress or a blouse-and-skirt coordinate in cotton and other natural fabrics is the regular attire.

A long weekend in the cooler mountain provinces in the north would require warmer clothing.

LANGUAGE

Pilipino, based on Tagalog, is the national language. Most Filipinos, from the street sweeper to the nightclub hostess, speak English but don't expect perfect grammar and pronunciation. Many speak it with a heavy regional accent, depending on what part of the country they come from. The ability to speak good English generally depends on one's educational background, though some who find it particularly useful in their trade cultivate it even outside school.

The government has made recent attempts to encourage the use of Pilipino in official circles. And there are now more programs in the broadcast media using Pilipino. Still, the language of business is English, and it is perhaps safe to say that no amount of legislation can change this in the near future, mainly due to the exigencies of international trade.

It might be useful to know that the Philippines is composed of more than a hundred ethno-linguistic groups, and that language tends to be an emotional issue among rival groups. In many instances, the *lingua franca* for Filipinos coming from different regions and who can speak only their native dialects is English.

Most Manilans, although they may come from various regions, can speak Tagalog. Cebuano is spoken in Cebu and other provinces in the Visayas, and has probably about as many speakers, if not more, as Tagalog. Mindano is a babel of tongues. The people of Zamboanga City speak Chavacano, which is pidgin Spanish, while the various Muslim communities speak a host of languages depending on their ethnic origin.

"Mabuhay", literally "to live", is Tagalog for "Welcome" and "Long Live". You will often hear it spoken in greetings and toasts. "Salamat" is "Thank You". By popular usage, "Hi", "Hello", and "Bye" have become part of the Pilipino vocabulary. "Hello" is the first word you'll hear on the phone and no inventive Filipino has yet coined a word to replace it.

ACCOMMODATION

Most international hotel chains such as the Mandarin Oriental, Peninsula, Holiday Inn, Hyatt, Intercontinental, Sheraton and Ramada are represented in Manila. The majority of these are located in the business district of Makati and along Manila Bay in Roxas Boulevard. Other first-class hotels are the Manila Hotel, The Manila Pavilion (previously the Manila Hilton), Philippine Plaza, and The Regent of Manila. The average daily rate for a single room is US$95-100, for a double room US$120-140. Reduced rates are available during slack seasons, or through special agreements.

Cost-conscious visitors will find a wide range of less expensive hotels to choose from in Makati, Quezon City, Ermita (the tourist district), and Roxas Boulevard. Service is not the best in the world, but the basics are there: air-conditioned room, clean sheets, clean bathroom with running water, and a telephone that works. The amenities approach austere levels the lower down the scale you go. Security is more lax and you are more likely to be bothered by hustlers, fixers, and touts. If you are doing business in the Philippines, but are constrained by a budget, location should be your first consideration. Ask for advice from your travel agent or from the Philippine Embassy's tourist information center.

It is not unknown for foreigners to be approached by touts who loiter in hotel lobbies or corridors offering a choice of "earthly pleasures" and other services. First-class hotels implement strict rules prohibiting such solicitations but some manage to get round the dragnet. Be firm and say no. A first-time visitor to Manila should never tempt fate by venturing on unknown ground. Temper your curiosity with a dose of common sense and request to be taken around by people you have dealt with before.

For foreign businessmen who require accommodations for a longer stay, there are properties being rented out in the Makati district, from condominium and "apartel" units to houses in such exclusive villages as Forbes Park and Dasmarinas Village. Monthly rent depends on the facilities and location but would start at about P15,000. Those who work in Metro Manila would do well to find a place near their office, as traffic during rush hours can be extremely congested. Other prime locations in Metro Manila are Greenhills in Ortigas Avenue, and Roxas Boulevard.

BUSINESS HOURS

Government offices are open from Monday to Friday, from 8 am to 5 pm, with a one-hour lunch break. Some have adopted "flexible time", so it is wise to call first. Private offices work five and a half to six days a week, from 8 am or 9 am to 5 pm or 6 pm, with an hour's break for lunch. Many shops, grocery stores and big department stores do not close for lunch. Big commercial establishments are usually open on Sundays. Their work hours vary but average from 10 am to 6 pm. Banks are open from Monday to Friday, from 9 am through 4 pm.

The Philippines is eight hours ahead of GMT.

HOLIDAYS

The legal holidays in the Philippines are:

New Year's Day	1 January
Maundy Thursday	changeable
Good Friday	changeable
Labor Day	1 May
Araw ng Kagitingan	9 April
Maundy Thursdau	April 16
Good Friday	April 17
Black Saturday	April 18
Easter Day	April 19
Independence Day	12 June
National Heroes Day	25 August
Bonifacio Day	30 November
Christmas Day	25 December
Rizal Day	30 December

Special nationwide holidays:

All Saints Day	1 November
Last day of the year	31 December

Some holidays, including religious festivals, are celebrated only in specific localities, so be sure to check the dates if you are visiting areas outside Manila.

NAME CARDS

It helps to have some but the exchange of name cards has not taken hold in Manila as much as it has in Hong Kong or Taiwan, where offering one's name card has become as automatic as the handshake. It

101

is not unusual for name cards to be the last item on the agenda in a business meeting, unless you take the initiative. In the words of a manager of a big buying office:

> **❝** We are not very particular about name cards here. Frequently, when a foreigner gives a Filipino his name card, the latter does not have one with him. It might be in his drawer or somewhere else. He has one but it is not as readily available as it is in Hong Kong or Japan."

COMMUNICATIONS

Public telephones (red phones) are found in hotels and commercial areas, and require three 25-centavo coins. Unlike the practice in Hong Kong, where you can use a shop's telephone for free, most shops in Manila charge P2.00 (US$0.09) per call. Some restaurants allow customers to use the telephone free of charge. No area prefixes are required.

International calls can be done either through an operator or by dialing direct, but few private telephones have this function. You can call collect to most countries.

International courier and telecom companies are represented in Manila and should be used for important documents and parcels. Most hotels can arrange the posting for you. The Government Post Office is open from 8 am to 6 pm on weekdays and 8 am to 5 pm on Saturdays.

MEDIA

The leading English dailies are the *Manila Bulletin*, *Philippine Daily Inquirer*, *Daily Globe*, and the *Manila Chronicle* — which carries the bulk of employment ads in its Sunday issue. A new broadsheet in Pilipino, *Diyaryo Filipino*, recently came out with its first issue, backed by the same publishing group as the *Daily Globe*. In addition, there are tabloids in the local language, peddling mainly police stories interspersed with fillers of barely-clad women. These have long enjoyed brisk business. There are 26 English language dailies published in the Philippines.

Radio has the widest reach, with more than 200 commercial and non-commercial radio stations throughout the country. Manila has four commercial television stations and one government station, with relay stations in the provinces. Some hotels receive Far East Network (FEN) programs from Clark Air Force Base. Television is the most popular form of entertainment in areas with electricity. "Canned" programs are predominantly American.

FOOD

A quick lunch is available in local fast food centers or from Shakey's Pizza, Pizza Hut, McDonald's, Wendy's, and Kentucky Fried Chicken. Fast food centers, such as the one located in the basement of Shoemart Makati, offer greater variety with an array of food shops. Food is never hard to find in Manila and is available on street corners, in commercial centers, in hotels, and in office cafeterias. Standards of sanitation are dubious only in street stalls, otherwise food is generally clean and safe.

A great variety of food is found here — Filipino, Chinese, Western, Indian, and Southeast Asian. In recent years, Filipino food has become a hit among Manila's dining set. As a result, a profusion of restaurants serving Filipino food, as well as other cuisines, has emerged — in Pasay Road in Makati, in Morato Street and West Avenue in Quezon City, in the tourist belt, and along Roxas Boulevard. Seafood is especially recommended. A particularly enjoyable way of eating Filipino food is with one's hands. If you're aghast at the idea, you can ask for a spoon and fork.

Filipino dishes are closest in their ingredients and flavor to Southeast Asian food. Centuries of Spanish and Chinese influence have also left their mark on food, with some dishes being adapted to suit the palate of Filipinos. Common ingredients are pork, shrimps, fish, beef, chicken, and vegetables in such flavorings as soy sauce, coconut milk, vinegar or lime juice, tomato sauce, and peanut sauce. Restaurants serve a range of average and exotic varieties.

Chinese food is about as popular as Filipino food and available almost everywhere in Manila, but there is very little variety. Most Chinese restaurants serve Cantonese food. One or two odd Shanghainese or Sichuanese dishes may figure in the menu, but specialty restaurants featuring regional Chinese cuisine are rare. If you have the time, take your Chinese meal in Ongpin, the Chinese district. The assortment of shops and food stores, the cacophony of sounds, and the hustle and bustle are a sharp contrast to the sleekness of Makati.

Most prices in Manila's restaurants are reasonable compared to prices in similar establishments with the same standard of service and food in other parts of Asia. A typical meal for two ranges from

P250 to P350 (US$11 to $16). Top-class hotel restaurants are pricier. Most establishments automatically add on a service charge and a sales tax in the bill.

TIPPING

While tipping is an accepted practice, it is not mandatory nor is the price set. Most restaurants and hotels add on a service charge to the total amount, in which case an additional tip is entirely optional. A tip representing 10 percent of the total amount is fairly standard in restaurants. Porters and bellboys are also tipped, depending on the amount of accompanying baggage they carry for you.

SHOPPING

You can either go to the shopping centers or the markets. Shopping centers are complexes or massive, all-in-one structures that house shops, restaurants, grocery stores, movie houses and promenades. The major ones are the Makati Commercial Center, Greenhills Shopping Center, Araneta Shopping Center in Cubao, Quezon City, and Shoemart in West Avenue, Quezon City. Most prices are fixed. Markets offer generally the same merchandise as the shopping centers but here you can haggle and bring the price down. Be prepared to elbow your way through the sweaty crowds. The busiest ones are Quiapo, Baclaran, and Divisoria. For curios and souvenirs, visit Cartimar in Pasay City, south of downtown Manila, and Ermita, the tourist row. Pistang Pilipino near Roxas Boulevard is a sprawling flea market of Philippine products.

ENTERTAINMENT

Manila offers probably the richest choice of entertainment in all of Southeast Asia. You can listen, and dance, to music in bistros, hotels, and nightclubs, or sing-along. Filipino singers and musicians are among the best in Asia and the cream of the crop is still in Manila. If you're thirty-something, go to Bistro RJ in Makati or Quezon City for a nostalgic trip to the 1960s. Birdland in Quezon City has some of the best acts in town. Both charge about P100 (US$4.50) for entrance. If you're too tired to venture far, your hotel would possibly have something to suit your mood. Most hotels have music lounges with live music, lobbies where you can have a quiet drink while a solitary pianist plays in the corner. Discos are also found in hotels.

Roxas Boulevard is the nightclub row, featuring big bands, big dancing halls, and hostesses; the girlie bars are in the Ermita-Mabini area. Drinks are reasonably priced in these establishments but you might like to check any "surcharges" such as payment for the hostess's table time. They can be very expensive.

Gambling aficionados can go to the casino at the Philippine Village Hotel, the jai-alai fronton, the horse-racing course, or cockfights. The casino is open 24 hours a day, seven days a week, jai-alai is played nightly, but races and cockfights are scheduled.

Cultural shows and other theatrical fare featuring foreign and local performers are presented at the Cultural Center of the Philippines and the Metropolitan Theater. The Rajah Sulayman Theater at Fort Santiago stages original and translated plays in Pilipino. During daytime, you can visit museums and art galleries, among them the Ayala Museum in Makati and the Metropolitan Museum in Roxas Boulevard. The National Museum is near Rizal Park, in the old Congress Building.

UTILITIES

The power supply is 110 or 220 volts, AC60 cycles, but most houses and buildings use 110 volts. Baguio City and major hotels in Manila, Cebu, and Ilocos have 110-volt outlets. Your hotel can provide you with an adaptor if necessary.

Manila's water is potable but it would be wise to drink only boiled or bottled water. When outside Manila, don't take any chances. Drink only bottled water or soft drinks.

MEDICAL FACILITIES

Hospitals are either privately-owned, government-owned, or university hospitals. Facilities and services are good, particularly in well-known private hospitals, where many of the doctors are American-trained. One of the most reputable is the Makati Medical Center. Many top doctors combine hospital work with private practice. There is also a large number of private dentists.

A BRIEF HISTORY

Philippine history does not have any written records prior to the Spanish era. The Negritos, the dark-skinned Pygmies who lived by hunting, fishing, and food gathering and who are mentioned in history books as aborigines of the Philippines, are believed to have come to the islands via the land bridges between 30,000 and 25,000 years ago. These are the forebears of various tribes today known as Baluga, Atya, Agta, Aeta, Mamanuwa, Batak, Ata, and Ati.

The archipelago's location along the sea lanes used by trading vessels plying between Persia and the South China Sea made the islands a convenient stopping place for Indian, Arab, Japanese and Siamese merchants and adventurers.

The Philippines was the recipient of Indian cultural influence from the late 7th to 16th centuries via immigrants and traders from Indochina, Siam, Malaysia and Indonesia.

Written accounts in Chinese describe trade between China and the Philippines. Philippine products such as gold, pearls, tortoise shell, betel nut, edible bird's nest, cotton, and hemp were exchanged for silk and brocade textiles, colored beads, fans and umbrellas, porcelainware, bronze gongs, iron and tin.

Arab influence arrived at the end of 9th and early 10th century when Arab traders expelled from central and southern Chinese ports, sought a new route to obtain Chinese goods. Sulu, Palawan and Northern Luzon were on their route to Taiwan. Later Chinese Muslims and Mongols of the Yuan Dynasty (1279-1368) also traded with Sulu. It was not until the end of the 13th century that Muslim converts were made.

Trade with these Asian cultures and civilizations long antedated the first contacts with the West. Today, many aspects of Philippine life and culture show traces of these mixed influences.

Much of the Philippines' recorded history is colonial history. The country was colonized by Spain for more than 300 years (1565-1898) and then by the United States for 48 years (1898-1946).

Independence was granted by the United States on July 4, 1946, after a brief period of Japanese occupation, during which Filipinos fought side by side with the Americans. For a while after independence, the new republic celebrated Philippine Independence Day every July 4. But in a surge of national pride, this was eventually changed to June 12 in commemoration of the declaration of independence by the Philippine revolutionary government during their war of independence against Spain in 1898.

In 1898 Spain was on the brink of defeat at the hands of Filipino revolutionaries when it decided to cede the Philippines to the United

States. Spain had earlier agreed to hand over the city of Manila to the triumphant rebels, but unknown to them, it also struck a deal with the United States who agreed to intervene. In the handover which was formalized in the Treaty of Paris of December 1898, the United States became the second colonial master of the Filipinos.

The colonial experience has been jokingly likened by Filipinos to being in a convent for 300 years and being in Hollywood for the next 48 years. The most conspicuous institutions that America had bequeathed to the Philippines seemed to be the disco, the variety show and the beauty pageant.

While facetious, the statement captures the essence of Philippine life for 90 percent of its recorded existence and helps explain some of the bizzare and dissonant strains in Filipino culture.

For the greater part of its life as a republic, the Philippines has had a two-party system. Before President Ferdinand Marcos declared martial law in 1972, the two dominant political parties were the Nacionalista and the Liberal parties. Marcos, who was a Nacionalista, was elected president in 1966 and reigned as a virtual dictator from 1972, when he placed the country under military rule, until his ouster in 1986 in a show of "people's power".

The present president is Corazon Aquino, wife of the late senator Benigno Aquino, who was shot on his return to the Philippines after three years of exile in the United States. The late senator was Marcos's greatest political rival. He spent most of his life during Marcos's regime in jail. His widow, Corazon, was swept into the presidency by a tidal wave of mass protest against Marcos's dictatorship after the senator's death.

Massive corruption and influence peddling during the last years of Marcos's rule helped bring the Philippine economy to its lowest ebb in the post-war era. The first years of Aquino's presidency were rocked by coup attempts from a restive faction in the military and Marcos loyalists. This scared off prospective investors which the government was ardently wooing for much-needed hard currency. With the military finally firmly under control, the first signs of recovery were seen in 1991, when the country posted a 3 percent growth, largely consumer-led. But real recovery has yet to come. The government faces a daunting task as it tries to spark growth, and at the same time pay off the country's US$29.4 billion foreign debt, improve the living standards of 75 percent of the population still poverty-stricken, and battle an intractable insurgency.

The death of Ferdinand Marcos in Hawaii in September 1989 sparked a fierce debate in the Philippines. President Aquino refused to allow his body to be returned to his homeland for "national security" reasons while Marcos loyalists and others were claiming that burial in the Philippines was Marcos' constitutional right. At the time of going to press, the final resting place of Ferdinand Marcos was still under discussion.

OVERSEAS CONTACTS — PHILIPPINE TRADE OFFICES

Australia
Philippine Consulate General
Office of the Consul (Commercial)
Philippine Center
Ground Floor, 27-33 Wentworth
Avenue
Darlinghurst, Sydney 2010
Tel: (02) 2677500
Tlx: PTHSYD AA26382
Cable: PHILCONGEN SYDNEY

Belgium
Office of the Commercial Counsellor
Embassy of the Philippines
4th Floor, 130 Chaussee de la Hulpe
1170 Brussels
Tel: (02) 6723047
Cable: AMBAPHIL BRUSSELS

Canada
Philippine Trade Commission
60 Bloor St., West Suite 409
Toronto, Ontario M4W 3B8
Tel: (416) 9671788; 9671798
Tlx: 0622017 PTC TOR
Cable: PHILCONGEN TORONTO

China (People's Republic of)
Office of the Commercial Attache
Embassy of the Philippines
23 Xiu Shui Pei Jie
Jienkoumenwai, Beijing
Tel: 522794
Tlx: 22132 AMPHI CN

Denmark
Trade Office of the Philippines
International House, Bella Center

Center Boulevard
DK-2300 Copenhagen
Tel: 520211 local 261
Tlx: 31124 IHSTM dk
Cable: TRADE PHIL

France
Office of the Commercial Counsellor
Embassy of the Philippines
39 Georges Mandel Avenue
Paris 75016
Tel: 47551755
Tlx: PHCOMAT 640047F
Cable: AMBAPHIL PARIS

Germany
Office of the Commercial Attache
Embassy of the Philippines
Argelanderstrasse 1
5300 Bonn 1
West Germany
Tel: (228) 214704
Tlx: 8869571 PHBN D
Cable: AMBAPHIL BONN

Hong Kong
Office of the Trade Attache
Philippine Consulate General
21/F, Wah Kwong Regent Centre
88 Queen's Road, Central
Tel: 5-8100770; 5-235524
Tlx: 6543 DOTRP HX
Cable: PHILHOUSE HONGKONG

Indonesia
Office of the Commercial Attache
Embassy of the Philippines
Jalan Imam Bonjol 6-8

Jakarta
Tel: 3100197
Tlx: 61710 DTIREP 1A
Cable: MINTRADE JAKARTA

Japan
Philippine Consulate General
4th Floor, Taiwa Building
18-1 Akashi-machi Chuo-ku
Kobe
Tel: (078)339471
Cable: PHILCONGEN KOBE

Netherlands
Philippine Trade Promotion Centre
c/o CBI
P.O. Box 30009
3001 DA Rotterdam
Tel: (010)4330661
Tlx: 27064 TPO RM NL

Saudi Arabia
Commercial Department
Embassy of the Philippines
P.O. Box 9113, Jeddah 21413
Kingdom of Saudi Arabia
Tel: 6600348
Tlx: 6051054 PHILFN SJ
Cable: AMBAPHIL JEDDAH

Singapore
Office of the Commercial Attache
Embassy of the Philippines
20-B Nassim Road
Tel: 7373977, 7373754, 7373332,
7373293
Cable: AMBAPHIL SINGAPORE

South Korea
Office of the Commercial Attache
Embassy of the Philippines
No. 509-510 Yeoksam Dong
Kangnam-ku, Seoul
Tel: 5667133; 5686141
Tlx: PHILCOM K32451
Cable: PHILCOMATTACHE SEOUL

Spain
Embajada de Filipinas
Calle Claudio Coello 92
28006 Madrid
Tlx: 41276 AMFIL E

Switzerland
Office of the Commercial Counsellor
Philippine Mission to the United
Nations and other International
Organizations
42 Avenue Blanc, 1202
Geneva
Tel: 325964
Tlx: 289010 DBGV CH

Thailand
Office of the Commercial Attache
Embassy of the Philippines
760 Sukhumvit Road
Amphur Phra Kanong
Bangkok
Tel: 3910008; 3910211
Cable: AMBAPHIL BANGKOK

United Kingdom
Office of the Commercial Counsellor
1A Cumberland House
Kensington Court
London W8 5 NX
Tel: (01) 9371898
Tlx: 28161 PCOMAT G
Fax: 01-937-2747

United States
Office of the Philippine Trade
Representative
Philippine Consulate General
Suite 1909, 30 North Michigan
Avenue
Chicago, Illinois 60602
Tel: (312) 2363676; 9678847
Tlx: 6974831 PTO CGO
Cable: PHILCOMAT CHICAGO

CHAPTER 7

SINGAPORE

Getting there ■ Entry and exit formalities ■ Climate and attire ■ Hotels ■ Getting around ■ Tipping ■ Business hours ■ Smoking ■ Littering, jaywalking and other offenses ■ Drugs ■ Eating out ■ Night life ■ Sightseeing ■ Shopping ■ Medical facilities ■ Media ■ Electricity ■ Holidays ■ A brief history ■ Singapore contacts overseas

SINGAPORE

SINGAPORE HAS AN unenviable reputation for dullness. But while the night life is by no means as garish as it is in Bangkok and the sightseeing possibilities are more limited than in Malaysia or Indonesia, there are things to do and places to see both before and after dark. Indeed, it would be a terrible waste to spend the nonbusiness hours of a buying trip in your room, watching the hotel video channel. Singapore may be run by one of the more prudish governments in Asia — laws banning "immoral" pop records and the mildest of soft-porn sex magazines and movies are rigorously enforced — but you can still enjoy yourself there.

How did Singapore earn its image as the most boring city in Southeast Asia? It goes back to the late 1960s when Singapore became a licentious resort for American soldiers on R&R from Vietnam. Former prime minister Lee Kuan Yew and his People's Action Party (PAP) decided to clean up Singapore. They did a thorough job of it. The death penalty was — still is — enforced for morphine and heroin trafficking and stiff fines were introduced for littering and other antisocial behavior. Many of the city's bars, night clubs and massage parlors were closed, while all movies, records, magazines, newspapers and books deemed to be morally or politically offensive were banned. Men were required to wear their hair short and visiting hippies were intercepted by immigration officers and put on the next plane out.

After a while, the Singapore government's social engineering policies became so moralistic and restrictive that creative people left the country in droves. Tourism fell because of the lack of night life — Bangkok was much more fun — and by the early 1980's Singapore really was a bore. But things have changed lately. Notes one Singapore resident:

 There has been a proliferation of massage parlors in the last few years. They call themselves health clubs and they are low-key. The government knows what is going on, but tolerates it as long as it is not too blatant. It has to if it wants to attract tourists and business travelers."

Among the benefits of the big cleanup were the elimination of most of Singapore's industrial and sewage pollution, and the creation of a green, well-kept garden city where one can walk the streets at any time of the day or night without fear of being mugged. It is to be hoped that these gains, along with the city's international competitiveness as a business center, will not be lost as Singapore loosens up.

Singapore's economic success has created a new young middle class and this has led to the arrival in the last few years of a number of new yuppie bars, discos and restaurants. Meanwhile, Goh Chok Tong, Singapore's new prime minister, has appointed a minister of culture in a bid to promote the arts and to encourage young writers, artists and musicians to express themselves freely. Although it still has some of the world's harshest censorship laws, Singapore is gradually becoming livable as well as decent again.

GETTING THERE

Slowly but surely, Singapore is moving ahead of Hong Kong as the premier airline hub for Southeast Asia. Several major carriers — including Lufthansa, Swissair, Qantas and Japan Airlines — have increased the frequency of their services to Singapore recently. Meanwhile, Singapore Airlines (SIA), the nation's flag carrier, has become one of the world's 15 biggest airlines, serving a total of 63 destinations in 37 countries. It has invested in a fleet of Boeing 747-400 Megatop aircraft to serve such long-haul destinations as Los Angeles, San Francisco, Toronto, Frankfurt, London, Paris, Zurich, Rome, Amsterdam and Vienna. Singapore's Changi, generally considered to be one of the world's finest airports, has doubled its capacity by opening a second passenger terminal. The airport is linked to 110 cities through more than 2,100 flights a week.

ENTRY AND EXIT FORMALITIES

Holders of North American and west European passports do not require **visas** to enter Singapore for visits lasting up to 14 days. However, entry visas are required of visitors from India, the Soviet Union, China, Afghanistan, Cambodia, Laos, Vietnam, Algeria, Libya, Tunisia, Iraq, Kuwait and Lebanon. Yellow fever **vaccination certificates** are required of travelers from Africa and South America. As for **customs formalities**, there is no restriction on the amount of currency you can take into or out of Singapore. Duty-free concessions include 1 liter of spirits and 1 liter of wine. There are no concessions for cigarettes, however. Indeed, as part of the Singapore government's anti-smoking campaign, travelers are "fined" S$17 for each carton of cigarettes they take into the country.

Among the controlled and restricted items are compact discs, audio and video cassettes, which require a permit from the Ministry of Communication and Information's Board of Film Censors. Telecommunication and radio communication equipment has to be authorized by Singapore Telecom. Controlled drugs, reproductions of copyright publications, tapes and discs, endangered species of wildlife and their byproducts, obscene articles and publications, and seditious and treasonable materials are prohibited. The **airport departure tax** is S$12.

CLIMATE AND ATTIRE

Just 1 degree north of the Equator, Singapore is hot and humid all year round. Temperatures are generally around 30 degrees Celsius at noon and 23 degrees at night. The humidity is usually in the high 80's, but sea breezes and the large number of trees in the city mean the atmosphere is not as oppressive as in Taipei or Hong Kong. November to January is the wettest period because of the northeast monsoon, but there is some rain every month of the year. Short, sharp showers are not unusual early in the morning or in the evening. They come as a welcome relief, for they are followed by at least a few minutes of coolness.

Despite the heat, it is wise to carry a jacket or a light sweater to defend yourself against the ferocious airconditioning in offices, shops, restaurants and bars. As in Hong Kong, the owners and managers of many establishments appear determined to freeze their customers to death by making them sit in Arctic conditions. While you will never be ejected from a night spot for dressing up, only a few establishments insist on formal wear. As for business attire, there are four spheres in Singapore. The most formal is the Shenton Way financial district, where the men wear dark suits no matter how hot it is. In the Orchard Road area, however, it is quite acceptable to dispense with a jacket, although men are expected to wear a business shirt, tie and smart trousers. Shirt sleeves and an open collar are normal attire on the industrial estates. Perhaps surprisingly, officials in government departments and agencies usually dress informally, although a senior official may wear a tie. Government officials do not usually bother with suits, except on important occasions.

HOTELS

Singapore is extremely well served with international-class business hotels, most of which are concentrated in the Orchard Road area. However, some of the world's most spectacularly modern hotels — the Marina Mandarin, Oriental Singapore, Pan Pacific, Westin Plaza and

Westin Stamford — have gone up in the Raffles City area during the last few years. The Marina Mandarin and the Pan Pacific both feature breathtakingly beautiful, soaring atrium-type lobbies and are models of pushbutton, automated efficiency. Nearby is the stately Raffles Hotel, which was frequented in its heyday by heads of state, movie stars and authors including William Somerset Maugham and Rudyard Kipling. Kipling gave the Raffles a somewhat wry endorsement, noting:

> 66 Providence conducted me along a beach in full view of five miles of shipping — five solid miles of masts and funnels — to a place called Raffles Hotel, where the food is as excellent as the rooms are bad. Let the traveler take note. Feed at Raffles and sleep at the Hotel de l'Europe."

The Raffles had the last laugh, however, for the Hotel de l'Europe was later pulled down and replaced by Singapore's Supreme Court. There was talk a few years ago of demolishing the Raffles too. But the government stepped in to declare it a national monument. Now it is looking as good as it ever did thanks to a two-year-long renovation project costing some US$94 million. The hotel reopened in September 1991.

Good business hotels in the Orchard Road tourist area include the Dynasty, Meridien, Mandarin Singapore and Singapore Hilton on Orchard Road; Goodwood Park, Hyatt Regency Singapore, Melia at Scotts, Royal Holiday Inn Crowne Plaza and Sheraton Towers (Scotts Road); Boulevard (Orchard Boulevard), Holiday Inn Parkview (Cavenagh Road), Omni Marco Polo (Tanglin Road), Regent of Singapore (Cuscaden Road) and Shangri-La (Orange Grove Road). The most distinctive of these are the Goodwood Park, which almost rivals the Raffles in terms of age and ambience, and the Dynasty, an unusual Chinese-style property with a huge, ornate lobby. The others are modern, no-nonsense Western-style business hotels.

GETTING AROUND

Unlike most Southeast Asian cities, Singapore is well organized and safe. It is easy to get from the airport to your hotel. You will not have to fight your way through surging, sweaty throngs, nor will you be badgered by jewelry store touts and massage parlor pimps as you head for the exit. You will join an orderly queue for your taxi and, unless the airport is unusually busy, you will not have to wait more than a few minutes for a cab. The journey to your hotel will take about 25 minutes. The driver will not attempt to overcharge you, nor will he try to drive you to some remote spot and rob you at knifepoint.

The taxis in Singapore are as clean and efficient as everything else in the city. There are plenty of them, they are cheap and the drivers do not expect tips. You should not normally pay more than the amount displayed on the meter. However, there is a S$3 surcharge for journeys from the airport and a S$5 "fine" for using the Central Business District (CBD) at peak times (7.30 to 10.15 am and 4.40 to 6.30 pm). There is also a 50 percent surcharge for using a taxi between 12 midnight and 6 am. Cabs are supposed only to pick up passengers at marked taxi stops, but they can be flagged down almost anywhere in the city. You may consider using the Mass Rapid Transit (MRT) subway system to get to Jurong and some of the other industrial areas. Opened in 1987, the system is extremely clean, fast and efficient. The stations and platforms are clearly marked in English, while the ticket vending machines even give change.

TIPPING

As the giving and accepting of tips is prohibited at the airport and strongly discouraged by the government elsewhere porters, bellhops, waiters and taxi drivers do not expect them. Restaurants, bars and night clubs usually levy a 10 percent service charge.

BUSINESS HOURS

Government and private sector offices work from 9 am to 5 pm Monday to Friday and from 9 am to 1 pm on Saturdays. However, there is a growing trend toward a five-day week in the private sector. Banks open from 10 am to 3 pm Monday to Friday, and from 11 am to 4.30 pm on Saturdays.

SMOKING

The Singapore government is moving to a point where smoking will be totally illegal. It is already banned in taxis, on buses and the MRT, in government buildings, airconditioned restaurants, shopping centers and cinemas. Stiff fines are imposed for smoking offenses. On top of this, many hotels have nonsmoking floors, while other private establishments have introduced their own smoking bans. You can still smoke — owner permitting — in open-air restaurants and in bars when food is not being served. It is legal to smoke in the street, although tossing a cigarette butt into the gutter could land you with a heavy fine for littering.

LITTERING, JAYWALKING AND OTHER OFFENSES

Dropping litter, jaywalking, spitting or neglecting to flush a public toilet, are social "crimes" that can get you into big trouble in Singapore, for the fines for such misdemeanors are not petty. Many visitors find such rules and regulations to be pretty irritating, a restriction on self-expression and personal liberty. Most Singaporeans, however, accept them quite happily. Raised on the Confucian concept of respect for authority, they cannot understand why someone should expect to be able to drop garbage all over the place and get away with it. Nor do they see why people need to express themselves by depositing their saliva on the sidewalk. And they are baffled by those who are too lazy to walk an extra few yards to use a pedestrian crossing or too impatient to wait for the traffic lights to change.

DRUGS

The message to would-be drug traffickers is: don't even think about it. The death penalty is imposed for trafficking in more than 15 grams of heroin or more than 30 grams of morphine. For handling smaller amounts, jail sentences of 20 years or more, plus canings, are imposed. Any person trafficking in cannabis in excess of 10kg faces 20 to 30 years in jail, plus 15 strokes of the rotan cane. For possession or consumption of cannabis, there is a maximum of 10 years in jail and/or a fine of S$20,000. It is imperative for any traveler to Singapore, therefore, to reject any requests from others to check in or carry their baggage. It is also important to make sure your check-in luggage is locked and to keep a close eye on your carry-on bags.

EATING OUT

One big advantage Singapore has over Hong Kong and many other Asian cities is that you can still dine alfresco there and be reasonably sure you will not spend the night throwing up — or worse. Strict hygiene laws are enforced at all eating establishments, which means you

117

do not have to go to expensive restaurants every night to stay healthy. If you have the opportunity to eat at one of Singapore's outdoor food or "hawker" centers, take it. The food is excellent and cheap, and visiting one of these centers is a good way of getting to know and understand the local people. The Newton Circus food center, near Orchard Road, is popular with Singaporeans and tourists alike. Another good location for alfresco eating is the Cuppage Centre in Cuppage Road, off Orchard Road.

There is a comprehensive selection of more upscale restaurants in Singapore, many of the best of which are to be found in the international hotels. Good seafood restaurants enjoy the highest prestige and choosing one of these will certainly impress a status-conscious Chinese business client. The choice of Chinese cuisines in Singapore includes Beijing, Cantonese, Hokkien, Hunan, Szechuan and Teochew. There are also Malay, Indian and Nonya restaurants. Nonya cuisine combines elements of Malay and Chinese food and can be sampled at Peranakan Place, an interesting leisure complex on Orchard Road housing restaurants, bars, shops and a museum. Singapore also offers vegetarian, Thai, Indonesian, Indian, Vietnamese, Japanese, Korean and French restaurants. For the truly desperate, there are also some pseudo Mexican and Italian restaurants, while the city has seen a proliferation of Western-style fast food joints serving hamburgers, pizza or fried chicken.

NIGHT LIFE

Anybody who tells you Singapore is dead after dark is thoroughly mistaken, for there are plenty of lively bars and discos to choose from in the Orchard Road area. This may not be Bangkok — there are no nude dancing or live sex shows — but you can still have a good night out. The bars in Singapore are generally far more fun, and better value for money, than the overrated establishments Hong Kong has to offer. It is possible to spend an entire evening bar-hopping in one building. A shopping center by day, the Orchard Towers building at the Tanglin Road end of Orchard Road turns into a complex of bars and discos after dark. Among these are Caesars, where the waitresses wear togas; Top Ten, a skyscraper-theme disco; Ginivy's, which features live country music; and Club 392, where you can hear local rock bands.

Another good spot is the Shaw Centre at the junction of Scotts Road and Orchard Road. This houses the Jockey, a small, smoky British-style saloon bar popular with expatriates. It is adjoined, somewhat incongruously, by Einstein's, a yuppie bar and venue for local blues, reggae and rock bands. Another yuppie bar is Brannigan's, in the basement of the Hyatt Regency on Scotts Road. This too offers live rock music. HPL House, on Cuscaden Road, off Orchard Road, is a popular yuppie hangout, accommodating Singapore's branch of the Hard Rock Cafe chain and also Blue Moon, a "lifestyle" store which is recommended for its trendy fashion wear and unusual range of bootleg blues, jazz and rock compact discs.

Live rock, blues and jazz can be heard at the Saxophone, a small pub restaurant in Cuppage Road, near the Holiday Inn Parkview. Not far from this, at Peranakan Place, is Bibi's Theater Pub, a venue for a variety of local entertainers. The Warehouse, next to the River View Hotel on Havelock Road, is Singapore's biggest disco, having been created from two converted warehouses. Thank God It's Friday, a disco at Far East Plaza on Scotts Road, opens at 12 noon, every day. Like most of Singapore's better nightspots, it stays open until 2 am or later.

SIGHTSEEING

All of Singapore's major hotels offer sightseeing tours. Popular tourist haunts include the Botanic Gardens, Chinatown, Little India, Arab Street, Mount Faber, the Jurong Bird and Crocodile Park, Singapore Zoo, the Malay Cultural Village, and Chinese, Buddhist and Hindu temples. The average city tour, taking in Chinatown, the Botanic Gardens and Mount Faber — which affords a spectacular view of Singapore — lasts half a day. Ferry trips can be taken to the islands of Sentosa and Batam, and there are bus tours to the state of Johor in Malaysia. One of the more unusual tours is of one of Singapore's public housing estates. Independent types are recommended to consult "Tour it Yourself", a free walking tour guide published by the Singapore Tourist Promotion Board.

SHOPPING

Singapore is a shopper's paradise, competitive with Hong Kong in terms of both choice and prices. Apart from some egregious tailors in the big shopping centers, the shop assistants are generally more polite and knowledgeable than in Hong Kong. The shops are generally open from 10 am until 9 pm seven days a week (Tang's, a big department store on Orchard Road, is a notable exception, closing on Sundays for religious reasons). The practice of bargaining has largely disappeared, although some haggling is expected at the gold and jewelry dealers' centers on South Bridge Road, and also in Chinatown, Little India and Arab Street, where jewelry, batik ware and handicrafts are on sale.

Big shopping centers in the Orchard Road district belt such as Lucky Plaza, Forum Galleria, Scotts Shopping Centre and Far East Plaza are good for jewelry, watches, electrical goods and apparel. All of the prices are fixed, but some shopkeepers are inclined to bargain. Most of the shopping complexes house one or more licensed money changers. You can bargain with these to obtain exchange rates that are competitive with the banks' and far better than those offered by the hotels. Some shopping centers, such as the Delfi Orchard, Wisma Atria and Palais Renaissance, specialize in high-end branded fashion goods and are patronized largely by Japanese tourists.

MEDICAL FACILITIES

It is easy to buy aspirin, cough medicine, sticking plaster, etc., in hotels and at pharmacists. The latter are open from 9 am to as late as 10 pm. Good hotels have doctors on 24-hour call. Singapore's hospitals, doctors and dentists are reputed to be among the world's best.

MEDIA

There are two local morning English-language newspapers, the *Straits Times* and the *Business Times*. Local and Malaysian English-language television channels can be viewed. Hotels also offer CNN and teletext. The BBC World Service is broadcast on FM radio.

ELECTRICITY

The voltage is 220-240 volts AC, 50 cycles. Transformers and adapters for portable computers, electric shavers and hair dryers are easy to find at the local shopping centers.

HOLIDAYS

The national holidays combine both Western and Asian customs. Government offices, banks and many commercial establishments are closed on these days. Festivals based on the lunar calendar, marked with an asterisk (*) on the table below, vary from year to year.

Public holidays 1992

New Year's Day	January 1
Chinese Lunar New Year	February 5 *
Good Friday	April 17 *
Hari Raya Puasa	April 4-5 *
Labor Day	May 1
Vesak Day	May 17 *
Hari Raya Haji	June 11 *
National Day	August 9
Deepavali	October 26 *
Christmas Day	December 25

A BRIEF HISTORY

From trading outpost to major entrepôt

The history of Singapore is dominated by two remarkable men -- Sir Stamford Raffles, a farsighted empire-builder who annexed the island for Britain in 1819, and Lee Kuan Yew, a Cambridge-educated lawyer who was only 35 when he took charge of Singapore in 1959 and who stayed as prime minister for more than 30 years. Recognizing that Singapore's strategic location on the Straits of Malacca could make it one of the world's busiest ports, Raffles claimed the island as a trading settlement for the East India Company. In doing so, he defied protests from the Dutch, another seafaring nation competing with Britain for colonial booty in Southeast Asia. Raffles called Singapore "a child of my own". He wrote:

 It is impossible to conceive a place combining more advantages... already a population of above five thousand souls has collected under our flag, the number is daily increasing, the harbour, in every way superior, is filled with shipping from all quarters...Our object is not territory but trade, a great commercial emporium...and what Malta is in the west, that may Singapore become in the east."

Business was good from the start. Some 3,000 ships called at Singapore in its first three years as a British colony. By 1821, the population had reached about 5,000. It included immigrants from Europe, the Middle East, Armenia, India and China, but about 60 percent of the population then was made up of indigenous Malays. The Chinese, however, had become the biggest community by 1830, seven years

after Raffles had left Singapore (he died in 1826). As Raffles anticipated, Singapore had put older Malay settlements like Malacca and
Penang in the shade by the second half of the 19th Century. The
island realized its vast potential as an entrepôt as a result of the
invention of the steamship and the opening of the Suez Canal. Chinese immigration increased tremendously. In one year alone, 1912,
some 250,000 Chinese arrived, largely to take part in the booming
rubber trade.

The trauma of war and its aftermath

Thirty years later, however, things went horribly wrong for Singapore.
The complacent but ill-prepared British forces were overwhelmed by
the Japanese sweeping south from Malaya. On the eve of Chinese
New Year in 1942, Singapore surrendered. Sir Winston Churchill
called the fall of Singapore "the worst disaster and the largest capitu-
lation in British history". Singapore was ruled by the Japanese until
August 21, 1945. It was a deeply traumatic period and photographs of
the sufferings of prisoners of war and civilians are still on permanent
display in Singapore.

Singapore became a crown colony under a British governor after
the war, but soon began moving toward independence. A new constitution resulted in elections in 1955 to choose a chief minister and a
32-member legislative assembly. The pro-British Progressive Party
won only four seats, while the Labour Front, with 10, supplied
Singapore's first chief minister, David Marshall. He resigned the following year when Britain would not agree to full internal self-government. His deputy, Lim Yew Hock, took over for the next three years, a
period when Singapore was wracked by communist-inspired riots.
Lim negotiated agreement to self-government in 1958, but it was the
People's Action Party (PAP), led by Lee Kuan Yew, that swept to power
the following year.

Lee has said it was the Japanese occupation that made him a
politician and gave him a sense of nationalism. Ironically, he was
unable to put his nationalistic ideas immediately into effect. Lee was
a socialist and the PAP's huge election victory -- it took 43 of the 51
seats in the assembly -- frightened investors away. Convinced that
Singapore could not survive on its own, Lee spent the next four years
negotiating a merger with the Federation of Malaysia. This was
achieved in 1963. But the next two years saw a series of violent race
riots between Chinese and Malays. Eventually, the Malaysian prime
minister, Tengku Abdul Rahman, decided he had had enough and, on
August 9, 1965, Singapore left the federation. Two years later, the
British announced they were withdrawing their forces, leaving Singapore to fend for itself.

On its own -- an Asian success story

It seemed disastrous to some at the time. Singapore had high unemployment and its housing and education were inadequate. Britain's military establishment was generating about 15 percent of an ailing economy. But in the event, being left to its own devices was the best thing that could have happened to Singapore. Urged on by Lee Kuan Yew and the PAP, the country pulled itself up by the boot straps, tripling its gross national product within 10 years. Before the end of the 1970s, the housing shortage had been overcome, workers were being imported from Malaysia because of a shortage of labor, and economic growth was running at an annual rate of 10 percent or more. The economy has continued to develop, apart from a short, sharp recession in the mid-1980s. Singaporeans can now realistically aim at matching the standard of living enjoyed by the Swiss.

It is a miraculous story. The man mainly responsible for it, Lee Kuan Yew, continued as prime minister until 1990, when he handed over the job to Goh Chok Tong. Lee, however, continues in the government in the role of senior minister and it is said that he is still really in charge of the country. A controversial figure because of his authoritarian style, Lee has cracked down hard on internal political dissent and banned local distribution of foreign newspapers and magazines for publishing articles critical of his government. Actions like these have not made Lee popular overseas, but he is a highly respected father figure at home. It is difficult to think of another head of government who has exercised so much influence over his country without developing a cult of personality. There are no statues of him, nor have any authorized biographies been published to glorify his deeds. He prefers to let his achievements speak for themselves. Even his harshest critics admit that without Lee Kuan Yew, Singapore would not have made it.

SINGAPORE CONTACTS OVERSEAS

Singapore Trade Development Board Offices

Head Office
1 Maritime Square
#10-40 (Lobby D)
World Trade Centre
Telok Blangah Road
Singapore 0409
Tel: 271 9388

Cable: SINTRADEV
Telex: RS 28617, RS 28170 TRADEV
Fax: 274 0770, 278 2518

Australia

Suite 907, Level 9
MLC Centre, Martin Place
Sydney NSW 2000
Australia
Tel: (61-2) 233 7015/233 3391
Fax: (61-2) 233 4361
Contact: Ng Chon Choo, Centre
Director

Britain

5 Chesham Street
London SW1X 8ND
United Kingdom
Tel: (44-71) 245 9709
Telex: 921117 STDBL G
Fax: (44-71) 235 9792
Contact: Tham Hock Chee, Centre
Director/First Secretary

Canada

c/o United Overseas Bank (Canada)
Suite 310 Vancouver Centre
PO Box 11616
650 West Georgia Street
Vancouver BC V6B 4N9
Canada
Tel: (1-604) 662-7055
Telex: 507520 TYEHUA VCR
Cable: TYEHUABANK
Fax: (1-604) 662-3356
Contact: Ng Chee Meng, Honorary
Trade Representative

China

Office of the Singapore Commercial
Representative — Beijing
4 Liangmahae Nanlu
Sanlitun
Beijing 100600
People's Republic of China
Tel: (86-1) 532 3926, 532 3143
Cable: SINGAWAKIL BEIJING
Telex: 22578 SINBJ CN
Fax: (86-1) 532 2215
Contact: Wong Heng San
Commercial Attache

Dubai

c/o Al-Futtaim Industries Pte Ltd
PO Box 152
Dubai
United Arab Emirates
Tel: 971-4 233 961
Telex: 45462 FUTAIM EM
    47730 INDUS X
Fax: 971-4 212 933
Contact: K.S. Stack, Honorary Trade
Representative

Germany

c/o Neptune Orient Lines
Kaiserstrasse 42
D-4000 Dusseldorf 30
Postfach 320526
Federal Republic of Germany
Contact: Patrick Soon, Honorary
Trade Representative

Hong Kong

Units 901-2, 9/F
Admiralty Centre, Tower 1
18 Harcourt Road
Hong Kong
Tel: (852) 528 6185
Telex: 66791 TDBHK HX
Fax: (852) 861 0048
Contact: Sng Sow Mei, Centre
Director/Counselor (Commercial)

India

88 A Jolly Maker Chamber II
Nariman Point
Bombay 400-021
India
Tel: (91-22) 204 0732
Telex: 11-86165
Fax: (91-22) 204 5051
Contact: Vaishnav Puri, Honorary
Trade Representative

Indonesia

Embassy of the Republic of
Singapore
Block X/4, Kav. No.2
Jl. HR Rasuna Said

Kuningan
Jakarta 12950
Indonesia
Tel: (62-21) 520 1476
Cable: SINGAWAKIL JAKARTA
Telex: 62213 SINGA IA
Fax: (62-21) 520 1488
Contact: Juliani Dipayuana, Trade
Assistant

Japan
c/o Consulate General of the
Republic of Singapore — Osaka
14th Floor, Osaka Kokusai Building
3-13 Azuchi-machi, 2-chome
Chuo-ku, Osaka 541
Japan
Tel: (81-6) 262-2662
Telex: 64596
Fax: (81-6) 262-2664
Contact: Goh Oon Tong, Centre
Director/Consul

Korea
c/o Ashin Shipping Co Ltd
Marine Centre, 10th Floor
52 Sokong-dong, Chung-ku
Seoul
Republic of Korea
Tel: 757 6944 (direct)/753 1211
Telex: ASHINCO K 24722
Fax: 757 4919
Contact: Bae Joo Wah, Honorary
Trade Representative

Saudi Arabia
c/o Consulate of the Republic of
Singapore
Suite 1021, 10th Floor
Corniche Commercial Centre
PO Box 18294
Jeddah 21415
Kingdom of Saudi Arabia
Tel: (966-2) 643 5677, 643 7267

Telex: 605794 TDBJED SJ
Fax: (966-2) 643 0750
Contact: Marah Hoessein Salim,
Centre Director/ Consul
(Commercial)

Sweden
c/o Consulate-General of the
Republic of Singapore — Sweden
Storgatan 42
11455 Stockholm
Sweden
Tel: (46-8) 660 0135
Fax: (46-8) 662 2035
Contact: Gunnar S.R. Wahlgren,
Honorary Trade
Representative/Honorary Trade
Consul

Switzerland
Permanent Mission of Singapore to
the United Nations — Geneva
6 Bis Rue Antoine — Carteret
1202 Geneva
Switzerland
Tel: (41-22) 447 330, 447 339
Cable: SINGAWAKIL GENEVA
Telex: 415909 SINGH CH
Fax: (41-22) 457 910
Contact: Yong Siew Min, First
Secretary (Economics)

United States of America
Los Angeles World Trade Center
350 South Figueroa Street
Suite 909
Los Angeles
California 90071
USA
Tel: (1-213) 617-7358/9, 617-7397/8
Fax: (1-213) 617-7367
Contact: Thian Tai Chew (Centre
Director)

CHAPTER

TAIWAN

Tourist information hot line ■ Visas ■ Air travel to Taiwan ■ Getting around Taiwan ■ Getting around major cities ■ Taxis ■ Rent a car ■ Accommodation ■ Physical exercise facilities ■ Entertainment ■ Night life ■ Climate ■ Currency and credit ■ Name cards ■ Tipping ■ Dress ■ Business hours ■ Medical care ■ Vaccinations ■ Public holidays ■ Local time ■ A brief history of Taiwan and its people ■ Telecommunications ■ Taiwan addresses overseas

TAIWAN

TOURIST INFORMATION HOT LINE

The Ministry of Information's Tourism Bureau offers travel information, emergency assistance, "instant" interpreting services and help for problems encountered by foreigners from 8 am to 8 pm every day. Just dial: (02) 717-3737. (No need to dial 02 if you are in Taipei.).

VISAS

All foreigners must have a visa to enter Taiwan. There are various types obtainable from ROC embassies, consulates or authorized representatives abroad. Multiple-entry and resident visas are available for certain purposes. The following are the four types normally issued to tourists and businessmen:

Transit: Must be used within three months of receipt. Valid for up to 14 days.

Tourist A: Must be used within six months of receipt. Valid for up to 30 days and can be extended for a further 30 days.

Tourist B: Must be used within three months of receipt. Valid for up to 60 days and can be extended for a maximum 120 days. People conducting business in Taiwan normally use this type of visa.

Entry: Valid for one entry for a period of six, 12 or 48 months depending on purpose of visit.

To extend a Tourist A or B visa, applications must be made to:

> *Foreigners Service Center*
> *Taipei Municipal Police Headquarters*
> *89 Ning Hsia Road*
> *Taipei, Taiwan*
> *Tel: (02) 5373680*

Special note: Taiwan visas are often not stamped in your passport (ostensibly because the country in question does not recognize the Republic of China), but are issued on a separate piece of paper. This sheet of paper is necessary for both entry and exit — so don't throw it away after you arrive in Taiwan! If you do misplace it, you are required to report the loss immediately to the Police Headquarters noted above. Should you be in a rush to depart, simply arrive at the airport and affect total surprise when asked for your visa — with luck, you'll be given a short lecture but allowed to board!

AIR TRAVEL TO TAIWAN

Taiwan has two international airports — the Chiang Kai-shek International Airport in Taoyuan, 30km from Taipei, and one down south in Kaohsiung. Over 15 airlines serve Taiwan, some operating direct flights to the United States and parts of Asia and Europe.

No matter what your ticket status is on arrival, **don't forget to confirm your flight** by telephone within 72 hours before departure. Seats are in high demand as the newly affluent Taiwanese now travel more than ever, and thousands leave each month for China via Hong Kong and Japan. Airlines — even international firms — will not waste a moment in reassigning your seat should you fail to reconfirm. Departure tax is NT$300 (US$10.66).

If you try to reconfirm with less than 24 hours to go before departure, you may be told point blank that your seat is no longer available. In such a case, there is only one remedy: take the first taxi available to the offices of the airline in question, and be prepared to argue until your seat is given back to you. If you proceed straight to the airport without reconfirming by telephone, the odds are very high you will not get on the plane — and your ticket will be invalid.

Peak seasons and destinations include December-January, when international travel is up and Taiwan's overseas college students take advantage of the holidays to visit their families from the United States; August-September when thousands of Hong Kong and Taiwanese students are US-bound for university studies; January-February, when thousands of Hong Kongers and Taiwanese take advantage of Chinese New Year to travel; and October, when trade shows in Korea, Japan, Taiwan, Hong Kong and China bring tens of thousands of businessmen to and through Taiwan.

Due to Taiwan's new policy of allowing its nationals to visit relatives in China, Hong Kong flights are hard to book at almost any time. One option is to switch your port of departure/arrival to Kaohsiung, which does serve Hong Kong but is almost never at full capacity. The bus or train ride up to Taipei takes four hours and is quite pleasant.

Avoid buying tickets in Taiwan if possible, as prices are markedly higher than in neighboring Hong Kong, and refunds on unused economy tickets can rarely be issued except to the ticket holder — in

Taiwan.

From C.K.S. Airport into Taipei, taxi fares are in the region of NT$1,000 (US$35.50) — if you get an honest taxi driver. Before taking a seat, make it clear whether you are paying an agreed upon fee, or paying the meter price. Foreigners are advised to avoid taking a taxi from the airport, as stories abound of unscrupulous drivers who "take you for a ride".

It is easy and more economical to use the Hotel Bus service offered by various hotels. The journey to a hotel in central Taipei will cost between NT$250 and NT$300. Hotel buses depart from the left hand side of the arrivals hall and there are normally uniformed men waiting to guide you. Even cheaper — costing NT$72 — are the local town buses (air-conditioned) which stop at about ten major hotels and terminate at the Taipei train station. Tickets can be obtained from the airport and bus drivers speak enough English to understand which hotel you are going to. Bus service to Taichung is also available right outside the arrivals hall.

GETTING AROUND TAIWAN

By Air

There are 12 domestic airports in Taiwan. These are in Taipei, Hualien, Taitung, Taichung, Tainan, Chiayi, Makung, Chimei, Lanyu, Lutao, Wangan and Liuchiuyu. China Airlines and Far Eastern Air Transport run flights from Taipei to these destinations. Taiwan Airlines and Formosa Airlines operate services between these airports and to the islands. For details and reservations, telephone:

China Airlines(02) 715-1122
Far Eastern Transport(02) 361-5431
Taiwan Airlines(02) 537-3660
Formosa Airlines(02) 536-4188

By Road

Taiwan's recent improvement of its roadway system, now totalling almost 20,000 km, has seen a vast percentage of travelers opting to travel by road rather than rail. The types of road are split into the north-south freeway, round-island, cross-island, vertical and coastal connecting roads. By Western standards, the only truly comfortable and efficient bus service is the four-hour ride between Taipei-Kaohsiung on the 4-8 lane superhighway, the Sun Yat-Sen Freeway. Routes between major cities on the west coast offer the optional luxury of air-conditioned coaches; many other less important destinations do not, but the scenery on winding east-west roadways is lovely.

By Rail
There are two railway lines operating in Taiwan — known as the East and West lines — covering 234 stations. The "Chukwang" and "Tsuchiang" are express trains and are comfortable and air-conditioned. Sleeping cars are available on trains running from Taipei to Kaohsiung. For further information, telephone the Taiwan Railway Administration (02) 311-0121. Getting a seat even at the last minute is rarely difficult.

GETTING AROUND MAJOR CITIES

There are numerous well-served bus routes which are convenient and cheap but crowded. Visitors tend to take the cheap and plentiful taxis, because bus routes are only marked in Chinese. But the adventurous foreigner armed with a Chinese address and willing to take a bus will definitely get where he is going, as the Taiwanese are overwhelmingly helpful.

TAXIS

Taiwan's taxi rates — like Hong Kong, Seoul, Bangkok etc. — are much lower than in the West. Even so, the days of the truly cheap taxi are long gone in Taiwan. As of early 1989, the first kilometer cost NT$35 (US$1.25) and NT$5 (17 cents) for each additional 400 meters, with an additional NT$5 for each five minutes in slow or stand-still traffic. A typical ride — even one that looks fairly close on a map — costs at least NT$75 (US$2.66) and takes 10-15 minutes.

Three items to consider: 1) English-speaking cabbies are few and far between, so ALWAYS bring a card with your destination written in Chinese; 2) When traveling within city limits, check to make sure the meter is running. If not, tell your driver immediately to flip on the meter, or be prepared to pay the price he sets when you arrive; 3) Cabbies don't like to run their meters when traveling outside the city, or late at night. You must be prepared to haggle over prices right at the beginning; making a quick exit after arrival without paying will be thwarted, as most cabs have doors which can be opened only by the driver, *not* the passenger. If you foresee such a case, remember to ask your host in advance how much you should expect to pay.

RENT A CAR

If you wish to drive yourself around Taiwan and maybe do some sight-seeing during your spare time, there are car rental firms open for tourist use. Highway signs are in Chinese and English, although few city street signs are bilingual. Rental fees per day start at around NT$1,200. For further details, call any of these numbers in Taipei: 882-1000; 831-2906; 500-6633; 713-1111.

ACCOMMODATION

Taiwan has a number of hotels with a large range of prices and facilities. There are few five-star hotels by international standards but some of the top-class ones in Taipei include the Lai Lai Sheraton, the Hilton, the Ambassador, the Howard Plaza and the Royal. Room rates for these hotels are in the region of NT$3,500 and NT$5,000 including surcharges.

Kaohsiung offers a limited range of hotels, the two leaders being the Ambassador Hotel and Hotel Kingdom. Typical room rates are less in other parts of the country — in Kaohsiung NT$1,433, in Taichung NT$1,076 and in Hualien NT$967.

For the economy-minded businessman, it is no problem whatsoever to find decently equipped rooms for one-half the cost of those listed above. But there are two points to consider: 1) Should your supplier visit you there, he may draw the conclusion that you are either an unsuccessful businessman, or a very cheap one; and 2) You are quite likely to be approached by hotel staff touting the services of a local call girl. A polite "No" will suffice to guard your privacy, however.

Hotels will accommodate appliances for 110 volts on 60 cycles AC.

PHYSICAL EXERCISE FACILITIES

Health-conscious executives take note: at least a dozen of Taipei's leading hotels have some kind of exercise facilities.

A brief rundown: body-building equipment, massage services and sauna rooms are common; most hotel guests need not pay for use of exercise equipment; Howard Plaza has **aerobics classes**; the Hotel Royal boasts a **swimming pool** as do the Ambassador and the Grand; Lai Lai Sheraton tops the list with a **rooftop jogging track**, **squash courts**, and **swimming pool**.

Other hotels with exercise facilities include the Grand, Gloria, Rebar Crown, Imperial, Ritz, Hilton, Asiaworld Plaza and Fortuna.

Frequent travelers to Taiwan may be interested in associate membership at the Clark Hatch Fitness Center (205 Tunhua North Road, Taipei. Tel: (02) 7137842 or 7127113).

ENTERTAINMENT

Dining out

Taking dinner outside your hotel is a treat, and fairly cheap. It appears that there are more restaurants per square foot in Taipei than anywhere else in the world — save Hong Kong. Unfortunately, Chinese food is *not* for the solitary diner, so invite someone along whenever possible.

All the traditional Chinese cuisines are available: Szechwanese and Hunanese (both rather spicy, unbearably so for some!), Cantonese (specializing in Hong Kong-style brunch), Shanghainese, Pekinese (Peking duck, hot pot for winter) and Taiwanese (less spicy, light and plenty of seafood). Japanese restaurants are numerous and good but usually very pricey. Full-service restaurants and cafes serving "Western" food are popping up all over Taiwan, but with the exception of those in top-class hotels, they aim to satisfy local tastes and may not be up to your standards. Meanwhile, fast-food from the West is taking the island by storm: McDonald's, Shakey's Pizzas and Kentucky Fried Chicken outlets are appearing "like mushrooms after a spring rain".

NIGHT LIFE

Taipei boasts a variety of Western, Japanese and Taiwanese forms of entertainment. Many of the venues are centered in the northwest part of the city, near the President Hotel off of Chungshan North Road. Western-styled discos, pubs and bars can be found in most major hotels as well. Service and standards of behavior are pretty much the same as in any international city.

Karaoke (sing-along) bars have hit it big here. Frequent travelers to Japan know karaoke bars are a good place to have a drink and get to know the locals — although sometimes frightfully expensive. Not so in Taiwan, where the drinks are reasonably priced. Karaoke (a sound system which combines your singing with pre-recorded but lyric-free music) is also an excellent opportunity to get to know your Taiwanese supplier. What could be more fun than singing along to your favorite tunes, microphone in hand as your image (caught by a video camera) is flashed on the wall for all to see? The one unwritten rule is that if your host sings, you too must sing a song. He who laughs must also be laughed at!

Chinese-style nightclubs abound, in Taipei and other cities. Traditionally, they have their own band and a large area for dancing, although some provide both "canned" (disco) music and live sets. Perhaps the most striking aspect to a foreigner is the presence of well-dressed, heavily made-up hostesses. They are dispatched to each table where they make conversation and dance with the guests, who pay what is known as "table-time", i.e., a set fee for her company during the evening. Good nightclubs are known for some of the best dancing — often something out of the 1930s or 1940s — in Taiwan.

Inevitably, some hostesses will end up leaving with willing guests, who pay the management a fee for their company which often extends through the night. Some foreigners find this practice offensive, and the Taiwanese have come to understand this over the years. Rarely will your host insist on taking you to such a club should you refuse his first invitation, but not going at least once is a chance lost to see another side of Taiwan.

For their part, hostesses are often fluent speakers of English or Japanese, perfectly used to entertaining mixed groups of single and married men and women in the nightclub. Assuming you can "let your hair down" and enjoy the atmosphere, a good time can be had by all.

CLIMATE

Taiwan is miserably humid all year-round, with humidity averaging 82 percent. The hottest weather is between April and November, when only light clothing is needed, temperatures averaging 24 degrees Celsius (75 degrees Fahrenheit) in Taipei. Typhoons and heavy thunderstorms are common during the summer months. Winter is between December and March. Temperatures do not normally fall much below 15 degrees Celsius (60 degrees Fahrenheit).

CURRENCY AND CREDIT

The official currency of Taiwan is the New Taiwan dollar (NT$). It is circulated in coins worth one-half, one, five and 10 dollars and in notes of 50, 100, 500 and 1,000.

Credit cards

American Express, Master, Visa and Diners Club cards are accepted in most shops, hotels and restaurants in Taipei, although sometimes a surcharge is added. Do not assume, however, that a credit card can be used — ask first. Until the end of 1988, banks in Taiwan were forbidden from issuing credit cards to Taiwanese. Now that the ban has been lifted, it should be increasingly easier to use credit cards in all major cities.

NAME CARDS

On every initial introduction it is customary to exchange name cards with the handshake. Virtually everyone in business circles has a name card and after a week's trip you will probably have accumulated a large handful. Be equipped with enough to see you through your trip — one hundred should suffice for one week.

TIPPING

In general, tipping is not expected in local bars and restaurants. However in international hotels, clients are expected to tip although surcharges are added on to bills. Taxi drivers expect a little extra, especially when assistance with luggage is given.

DRESS

During the summer months, it is acceptable for businessmen to wear short-sleeved shirts with their ties and suits. Formal dress is expected at business meetings. Socially, casual Western dress is accepted but it is advisable to avoid wearing shorts when dining out.

BUSINESS HOURS

Banks are open from 9 am to 3.30 pm Monday to Friday and 9 am to 12 noon on Saturday. Most commercial businesses operate between 9 am and 5 pm on weekdays and 9 am to 12 noon on Saturday. Lunch hours normally last between 12 noon and 2 pm. Government offices are open between 8.30 am and 12.30 pm, 1.30 pm to 5.30 pm Monday to Friday and 8.30 pm to 12.30 pm on Saturday.

Shopping arcades and department stores are open daily 10 am to 10 pm. Smaller shops normally close at 7 pm.

MEDICAL CARE

There are a number of private and public hospitals and clinics in all the major cities. Numerous drugstores provide light drugs as well as Chinese herbal medicine. For stronger drugs, a prescription is required.

It is not wise to drink water straight from the tap. Unless you plan to be in Taiwan for several weeks and want to build up resistance against local germs, avoid eating streetside vendors' goods.

VACCINATIONS

Visitors to Taiwan do not need any special vaccinations unless they are coming from an infected area, particularly with cholera.

PUBLIC HOLIDAYS

1992

Founding of the Republic of China	January 1 & 2
Chinese Lunar New Year (exact date changes annually)	February 4, 5 & 6
Youth Day	March 29
Tomb Sweeping Day and Death of President, Chiang Kai-sheck	April 5
Birthday of Matsu, Goddess of the Sea	April 28
Commemorates the landing in Taiwan on this day in 1661 of the Ming Dynasty loyalist, Cheng Cheung-kung	April 29
Dragon Boat Festival	June 8
Birthday of Cheng Huang, City God of Taipei	June 16
Chung Yuan Festival	August 15

Mid-Autumn Moon Festival	September 14
Confucius' Birthday	September 28
Double Tenth National Day	October 10
Overseas Chinese Day	October 21
Taiwan Retrocession Day	October 25
Birthday of President,	
Chiang Kai-shek	October 31
Dr Sun Yat-Sen's birthday	December 22
Constitution Day	December 25

LOCAL TIME

Taiwan is eight hours ahead of Greenwich Mean Time during the six winter months and seven hours ahead during the summer.

A BRIEF HISTORY OF TAIWAN AND ITS PEOPLE

The overwhelming majority of people living in Taiwan are of Chinese ancestry. The exception to this are the aboriginal peoples, now numbering only about 300,000, who were in Taiwan long before Chinese began migrating from Fujian Province. Speaking non-Chinese languages, many live in the less industrially developed areas such as Hualien and outlying islands such as Orchid Island and Green Island. According to Joseph Nerbonne, author of the comprehensive *Guide to Taipei and all Taiwan*, more than half of them still live in the mountains, while those in the lowlands have been pretty much Sinified.

Records show that Taiwan formally became part of the Chinese empire in the last years of the Yuan Dynasty, when the Mongols ruled China. By the time the Dutch invaded Taiwan in 1624, there were already 30,000 Chinese inhabitants. The Dutch stay was a relatively short one, ending 37 years later.

In 1895, the already critically weak Ching Dynasty ceded Taiwan to the Japanese as part of the price exacted for the Manchus' defeat in the Sino-Japanese War (1894-95). The Japanese occupied Taiwan until 1945, when the reins of power were passed to the Republic of China.

Chiang Kai-shek and the Nationalists retreated from the mainland to Taiwan in 1949, bringing some one million mainland Chinese with them. Chiang Kai-shek dominated the political scene as president until his death in 1975, followed by his son, Chiang Ching-Kuo, who died in January 1988. While the Kuomintang (KMT) still maintains an iron grip on power, opposition parties do now contest elections, the most high-profile being the Democratic Progressive Party.

Due to its unique history, Taiwanese culture today is an amalgamation of traditional Chinese, Japanese and modern Western ways of life. While the accent is clearly on "Chineseness", the Taiwanese are at home in an environment that contains elements of Japanese physical culture (old Japanese houses and tatami), aboriginal culture (handicrafts), and modern Western paraphernalia, from microcomputers to the Big Mac.

There are differences between the three types of Chinese in Taiwan: those who consider themselves truly "Taiwanese", being the descendants of Chinese who emigrated there hundreds of years ago; those who came from the mainland in the 1940s; and the latest generation, all of whom were born in Taiwan. Public education in a common language (Mandarin), constant social interaction and rapid economic progress benefiting virtually all parts of society have tended to blur these distinctions for the new generation, most of whom feel deeply rooted in Taiwan.

Language

The official language is Mandarin Chinese, which is pronounced the same way but written somewhat differently (using "traditional" characters) from the official language of China. The Taiwanese are educated in Mandarin and generally speak it in the workplace. But the vast majority of Taiwan's inhabitants, particularly outside of Taipei, speak the Taiwanese dialect (virtually the same as spoken in Xiamen City in Fujian Province) as a first language.

Japanese is widely spoken as a result of Japan's 50-year occupation (1895-1945) of the island, with the occasional older Taiwanese a more fluent reader of written Japanese than Mandarin. Trade ties and the popularity of "things Japanese" have kept general fluency in Japanese, even among younger Taiwanese, surprisingly widespread.

Virtually every Taiwanese under 40 has been taught English, but only those who use it on the job can actually speak it; in general, reading ability is much more common. Unlike in Hong Kong, you cannot expect your taxi driver to speak even basic English. Always have your destination written out in Chinese characters.

TELECOMMUNICATIONS

Telephoning overseas can be done either through the operator (dial 100) or by dialing direct, but few private phones have this function. For long-distance information in Taipei, call: 3212535. There are also public facilities for calling overseas at ITA offices (see below).

As Taiwan does not have agreements with some countries, including Hong Kong, it is not possible to call collect to those countries.

Local calls from public telephones are limited to three minutes and cost NT$1.00. To extend your conversation, keep another coin handy to drop in after the signal.

Cables and telegrams can be sent from ITA offices. The Taipei head office is located at:

28 Hangchou South Road
Section 1
Tel: (02) 3443781 (24 hours)

TAIWAN ADDRESSES OVERSEAS

Overseas branches and representative offices of the China External Trade Development Council:

Argentina
Oficina Comercial de Taiwan
Casilla No. 196
Av. Pte. Julio A. Roca 636, Piso 7
1067 Buenos Aires
1401 Capital Federal, Argentina
Tel: 307961, 307982, 308077
Telex: 23564 CCTROC
Cable: OFICOM TAIWAN BAIRES

Australia
Far East Trading Co., Pty. Ltd.
4th/Floor, International House
World Trade Center
Corner of Spencer and Flinders
Streets
Melbourne, Victoria 3005, Australia
Tel: (03) 6112988
Cable: FETRA MELBOURNE
Telex: AA 37248 FETR
Fax: 613-612983

Austria
Far East Trade Service, Inc.
Stubenring 4-12A
A-1010, Vienna, Austria
Tel: (0222) 5131933, 5131934
Tx: 116286 FETS A

Fax: (0222) 5137632

Belgium
Far East Trade Service, Inc.
World Trade Center 1, 16E etage
Boulevard Emile Jacqmain 162
Boite 33, 1210 Brussels, Belgium
Tel: (02) 2185157, 2185197
Cable: FAREASTRADE BRUSSELS
Telex: 25343 FETS B
Fax: (32-2) 218-6835

Brazil
Centro Comercial Do
Extremo-Oriente
Divisao de Promocao Do Comercio
Alameda Jau 1742, Conj. 101
CEP 01420, Sao Paulo
Brazil
Tel: (011) 2800151, 8810260
Telex: 112-5416 CCEO BR
Fax: (5511) 8837929

Canada
Far East Trade Service, Inc.
Suite 3315, 2 Bloor Street East
Toronto, Ontario M4W 1A8, Canada
Tel: (416) 9222412

Cable: FETSTOR TORONTO
Telex: 06528086 TROC TOR
Fax: (416) 9222426

Chile
Oficina Comercial del Lejano Oriente
La Gioconda 4222, Las Condes
Casilla 2-T, Correo Tajamar,
Santiago, Chile
Tel: 2282919, 2283185
Telex: 340412 PBVTR CK OFITAI
Cable: OFITAI SANTIAGO
Fax: (562) 2285854

Denmark
Far East Trade Office
Ny Ostergade 3, 1st/Floor
DK-1101, Copenhagen K
Denmark
Tel: (01) 123505
Cable: TREPRESENT
COPENHAGEN
Telex: 16600 FOTEX DK
Fax: 45-1-933916

France
Centre Asiatique de Promotion
Economique et Commerciale
3, Av. Bertie Albrecht, 6E Etage
75008 Paris
France
Tel: (1) 45633354, 45637900
Telex: 641275 F CAPEC
Fax: (1) 42660431

Germany
Taiwan Trade Service
Berliner Allee 61
4000 Duesseldorf 1, Germany
Tel: (0211) 84811
Telex: 8582232 FETS D
Fax: 211131790

Hong Kong
Hongkong Investment Liaison Office
415 Central Bldg
3 Pedder Street, Hong Kong
Tel: 5-243337

Cable: TSINGRICH HONG KONG

Indonesia
Chinese Chamber of Commerce of
Jakarta
No. 4, J1. Banyumas, P.O. Box 2922
Jakarta, Indonesia
Tel: 351212-4
Telex: 45126 SINOCH IA
Fax: (062) 021-3809063

Italy
Centro Commerciale Per L'estremo
Oriente
Via Errico Petrella, 2
20124 Milano, Italia
Tel: (02) 2853084
Cable: FAREASTRAD MILAN
Telex: 331594 BOFTTFI
Fax: 39-2-278077

Japan
Far East Trade Service Center
9-28, Hakata Ekimae 2-Chome
Hakata-Ku, Fukuoka, 812 Japan
Tel: (092) 4727461
Cable: FETS FUKUOKA
Fax: (092) 4727463

Korea
Office of Economic Counselor
Embassy of the Republic of China
83, 2-Ka, Myung-dong
Chung-Ku, Seoul, Korea
Tel: 7762889, 7575567
Telex: K27529 MEARO
Cable: SINOECON SEOUL
Fax: 002-82-02-7573859

Kuwait
Far East Trade Service, Inc.
P.O. Box 2590, 22026 Salmiya
Kuwait
Tel: 2418394, 2448225
Telex: 30674 FETS KT

Malaysia
Far East Trading & Tourism Center

SDN. BHD, Kuala Lumpur
Lot 202, Wisma Equity
150 Jalan Ampang, Kuala Lumpur
50450
Malaysia
Tel: (03) 2425549, 2426771
Cable: FOMLANDA
Telex: FETTC MA 30052
Fax: (03) 242-3906

Netherlands
Far East Trade Office
Economic Division
Javastraat 58, 2585 Ar., The Hague
The Netherlands
Tel: (070) 469552
Telex: 34281 ECODINL
Fax: (070) 600105

New Zealand
East Asia Trade Centre Auckland
Office
3rd/Floor, Norwich Union Bldg
Corner of Queen and Durham Streets
C.P.O. Box 4018
Auckland, New Zealand
Tel: (09) 33903
Cable: EASTRAD AUCKLAND
Telex: NZ 60209

Nigeria
Taipei World Trade Center
3rd/Floor, 24 Campbell Street
Lagos, Nigeria
Mailing address:
P.M.B. 12857 Marina
Lagos, Nigeria
Tel: (234) 1-6332783
Telex: 21030 TWTC NG
Fax: (234) 1-630615

Philippines
Pacific Economic & Cultural Center
P.O. Box 2043
Manila, Philippines
Tel: 461880, 472261-65
Cable: SINOECON MANILA
PHILIPPINES

Telex: 40417 PECCC PM
40434 EDPEC PM
Cable: SINOECON MANILA
Fax: 409713

Singapore
Trade Mission of the Republic of
China
in Singapore
460 Alexandra Road, #23-00 PSA
Bldg
Singapore 0511
Tel: 2786511
Cable: SINOMISION
Telex: RS 25438 SIMISON
Fax: 2789962

South Africa
Embassy of the Republic of China
Suite 1749, Sanlam Sentrum
Corner of Jeppe & Von Wielligh
Streets
P.O. Box 1148, Johannesburg 2000
Republic of South Africa
Tel: (011) 296335-8
Cable: SINOECON
Telex: 4-89808 SA
Fax: (011) 232236

Spain
Far East Trade Service S.A.
Torres De Jerez Planta 12-B
Torre II
Plaza De Colon No. 2
28046 Madrid
Spain
Tel: (91) 4101414, 4101513
Telex: 41633 FETSS E
Fax: (34) 1-4107314

Sri Lanka
Far East Trade Service Honorary
Representative
15, Kithi Yakara Road
Colombo 10
Sri Lanka
Tel: 91317
Telex: 21716 FRUKO CE

141

Attn: FETS
Office of the Economic Counsellor

Sweden
Taipei Trade Tourism & Information
Office
Wennergren Center, Sveavagen 166
4Tr. S-113 46 Stockholm
Sweden
Tel: (08) 7288523, 7288573
Telex: 15360 SHAMO S
Fax: (468) 7288584

Switzerland
Far East Trade Service, Inc.
Sihlquai 306
C-8005 Zurich
Switzerland
Tel: (01) 3634242-3
Cable: FETSI ZURICH
Telex: 817065 FETS CH
Fax: (01) 2717679

Thailand
Far East Trade Office
Economic Division
10th/Floor, Kian Gwan Bldg
140 Wit Thayu Road, Bangkok 10500
Thailand
Tel: 2519393-6, 2519274-6
Cable: CHINAIRTHA
Telex: 82184 CHINATA TH
Fax: 2535251

Turkey
Far East Trade Center
Buyukdere Cad. Oya Sok No. 109/11
Devran Apt. 6
Gayrettepe-Esentepe
Istanbul
Turkey
Tel: (1) 1750690
Fax: (1) 1663195

United Arab Emirates
Far East Trade Service, Inc.
P.O. Box 5852, Deira, Dubai, U.A.E.
Tel: 227388, 226537

Telex: 46717 FETSD EM

United Kingdom
Majestic Trading Co., Ltd.
5th/Floor, Bewlay House
2 Swallow Place
London W1R7AA
United Kingdom
Tel: (01) 6291516
Cable: MAJESCO LONDON W1
Telex: 25397 MAJECO G
Fax: (441) 4998730

United States
Economic Division, CCNAA
4301 Connecticut Ave., N.W.
Suite 420, Washington D.C. 20008
U.S.A.
Tel: (202) 6866400
Cable: SINOECO WASHINGTON
D.C.
Telex: 440292 SINOECO
Fax: (202) 3636294

Uruguay
Oficina del Agregado Comercial
Embajada de la Republica de China
Calle Dr. Jose Scoseria 2871 Bis Apt.
201
Mailing address:
Casilla de Correo 12173
Montevideo, Uruguay
Tel: 709459, 708711
Cable: SINOEMBASY
Telex: MEARO 22229

Venezuela
Oficina Comercial de Taiwan
Apartado 69149, Altamira, Caracas
1062-A
Venezuela
Tel: 328673
Cable: TAICOM CARACAS
VENEZUELA
Telex: 24619 TAICOM VE
Fax: (582) 310745

THAILAND

THAILAND

THAILAND HAS BECOME a popular destination for businessmen. Bangkok airport is on the stopover route of several of the world's major airlines and is the gateway to the rest of the nation. Doing a little homework on practical details — airlines, immigration, internal transport, health, climate etc., can ease your first encounter with the hustle and bustle of this crowded capital and assist your business trips to other areas of the country.

VISAS

Citizens of most nationalities are granted entry for 15 days on arrival in Thailand. Those wishing to stay longer than 15 days, must obtain a 60-day visa from a Thai embassy or consulate before embarking on their trip. This visa is extendible for an extra 30 days within Thailand for a cost of US$12. Those who do not extend their visas while in Thailand will be fined US$4 for each day spent in the country with an expired visa. Businessmen wanting to remain in Thailand for three months should obtain a non-immigrant visa which allows a 90-day stay. All visas should be used within 60 days of issuance unless an extension on the time of entry — up to six months — is granted by the Thai embassy. Airport tax on leaving Thailand is 150 baht (US$6).

For information on visa extensions, contact:

Immigration Division
Royal Thai Police Department
507 Soi Suan Plu
South Sathorn Road
Yannawa
Bangkok 10120
Tel: 286-7013-4

GETTING TO THAILAND

More than 50 airlines fly in and out of Bangkok to major cities all over the world. Thai International Airways is the largest airline and flies regularly to Europe, the Middle East, Africa and all over Asia. An hourly shuttle service operates from Hong Kong each day. Northwest and other large American airlines fly regularly to and from the United States. The main airport is Bangkok's Don Muang airport, situated about 22 kilometers west of the city center; this is the only airport in the capital. Chiangmai, in the north, and Phuket, in the south, are the next largest airports — both handling a direct service to Hong Kong. Other small airports are located in Koh Samui and U-Tapao, both in the south, and are only accessible via Bangkok airport.

GETTING FROM THE AIRPORT

A number of services are provided at Don Muang airport. Thai International Airways (*Thai*) has a counter opposite the exit from the customs area where vouchers for its services can be obtained. For those with a little extra to spend, the *Thai* limousines are air-conditioned and luxurious. To the city center they cost 400 baht (US$16.66) and operate round the clock. *Thai* also runs a shuttle to the City Terminal at the Asia Hotel for 60 baht (US$2.40). The shuttles leave at 30 minute intervals between 8 am and 8 pm. Taxis are also available at the airport, but beware of being overcharged — an average fare to the city centre is 200 baht (US$8), to be negotiated before the journey begins, not at its end.

GETTING AROUND THAILAND

DragonAir conducts a direct service from Hong Kong to the regional airports of Chiangmai and Phuket. Other international and national carriers serve these two airports and Koh Samui and U-Tapao, via Bangkok. Tickets are available from any travel agent or can be directly purchased from the airlines.

The major train lines run between Bangkok and Chiangmai in the north and to Pattaya and along the peninsula in the south.

One highway runs from Bangkok to Chiangmai and one from Bangkok to Hat Yai in the south. Hire car services are available and listed in the Bangkok Yellow Pages.

GETTING AROUND BANGKOK

Although public transport is readily available on the streets of Bangkok, the city is infamous for its traffic congestion, particularly during peak periods.

Taxis are easily flagged down on the streets and outside hotels. Because of the horrendous traffic jams, the taxis do not have meters — passengers must negotiate the price of a ride before climbing in and the driver sets a price according to the traffic. However, beware of being quoted too high a price. As with other Asian cities, most taxi rides here are fairly cheap but drivers are more than likely to add 30 percent onto the cost. It is wise to ask someone in your hotel to write the destination in Thai and advise you on the approximate price you should pay. Even in a rush hour the passenger should not pay more than about 70 baht (US$2.60) to get across the city. Public taxis have an illuminated taxi sign on their roofs — anyone who offers you a taxi ride in a car which does not have this is an illegal taxi driver and you are advised against riding with one. They are likely to offer to give you a guided sightseeing and shopping tour of Bangkok and charge an outrageous price. They call themselves **Private Taxis**.

Tuk-Tuks are a famous form of transport in Bangkok. They are three-wheeler motorized vehicles with flimsy roofs and no sides. They are not terribly comfortable and expose you to traffic fumes, but they are good fun. They are a slower form of transport and operate on the same sort of basis as taxis — a price must be negotiated before the ride. Rides cost a minimum of 20 baht (80 cents) and should be about half the price of taxis.

Buses run frequently and are even cheaper than tuk-tuks. However, they are not recommended as they are overcrowded and the destinations on the front tend to be in Thai.

River Taxis run along Bangkok's Chao Phraya river. These boats pick up passengers waiting along the piers and ferry them to various parts of the city for only three baht (1 cent)!

CLIMATE

Thailand has three seasons — hot and humid, warm and wet, and cool. The hottest and most humid time of year is between March and May when temperatures reach 41 degrees Celsius (106 degrees Fahrenheit) and humidity is over 90 percent. This combination of heat and humidity is intensified in the cities and is often uncomfortable for visitors not acclimatized to it. The rainy season is between June and October and normally sees rain for a period each day followed by brilliant sunshine at a very comfortable temperature. The rain can be extremely heavy and leads to flooding — and traffic chaos — in Bangkok. The cool season is when tourists are most comfortable, between October and February, when temperatures are around 25 degrees Celsius (in the mid-70s Fahrenheit).

PUBLIC HOLIDAYS

1992

New Year's Day	January 1
Makhabucha Day	February 18
Chakri Memorial Day	April 6
Songkran Festival Day	April 13-14
Labor Day	May 1
In lieu of Labor Day	May 2
Coronation Anniversary Day	May 5
Wisakhabucha Day	May 16
Bank mid-year Holiday	July 1
Asarnha Bucha Day	July 14
Buddhist Lent Day	July 15
HM The Queen's Birthday	August 12
Chulalongkorn Memorial Day	October 23
HM The King's Birthday	December 5
Constitution Day	December 10
New Year Eve	December 31

ATTIRE

Businessmen wear suits and ties and short-sleeved shirts are acceptable. Some businessmen wear safari suits in the hot season, but this depends on the business environment. Light clothing is worn all year round and there are no religious restrictions on dress in the streets. However, when visiting temples, everyone — particularly women — must cover their ankles and arms. Apart from upmarket hotel restaurants, any type of clothing is accepted in bars and restaurants.

BUSINESS HOURS

Government offices operate from 8.30 am to noon and from 1 pm to 4.30 pm on Monday to Friday; banks between 8.30 am and 3.30 pm.

on Monday to Friday; and shops from 9 am to 8 pm daily. Some companies work on Saturday mornings.

HEALTH

Visitors are advised not to drink tap water — only bottled water. Medical facilities in Bangkok are considered the best in the region, and a number of private and public hospitals are located in the city. Also, most hotels have an in-house doctor. No vaccinations are compulsory before entering Thailand, unless you are coming from an infected area. However, doctors tend to give a tetanus booster and typhoid and hepatitis vaccinations.

CURRENCY

The local currency is the baht which comes in notes of 10, 20, 50, 100 and 500 and in coins of 0.25, 0.5, 1, 2 and 5. Credit cards and travelers checks are widely accepted in cities around the country.

LANGUAGE

The Thai national language is, like Chinese, a tonal language and difficult for foreigners to understand. English is the second language and spoken in some form or another by most nationals, sometimes well in a business environment and not so well in rural parts.

LOCAL TIME

Thailand is seven hours ahead of Greenwich Mean Time.

COMMUNICATIONS

In all urban areas throughout Thailand, fax, telex, telephone and telegraphs are readily accessible. International direct dialling can be made from hotels but a surcharge is added. On other telephone lines, you must make overseas calls through an operator.

NEWSPAPERS

Two daily newspapers in English are published in all cities around the country. They are the *Bangkok Post* and *The Nation*. Most international newspapers and magazines are available from hotels and bookstores.

ELECTRICITY

The standard domestic voltage is 220 volts 50 cycles AC.

SHOPPING

Bangkok is a renowned "goldmine" for shoppers. Department stores, markets, and street stalls selling watches, jewelry, silk, leather, handicrafts, etc. are to be found in abundance. There is a weekend market selling all types of Thai products, the Siam Center has a huge complex of little shops, and River City contains rows of Thai silk shops. Patpong's night market is where most of the counterfeit Benetton, Cartier, Esprit, Rolex and other "famous brandname" products are sold. Prices are cheap but not as rock bottom for foreigners as for locals — the Thai vendors will always try their luck by charging at least twice the local price. No prices are put on market stall products and you are expected to barter for at least 30 percent less.

RELIGION

Ninety-five percent of Thais practice Buddhism. Sons of fairly orthodox families are required to devote a certain time to the temple, normally in their early teens. The other 6 percent of the population practice Hinduism, Christianity or Islam.

ACCOMMODATION

Bangkok has over 20 first-class hotels, such as the Oriental, the Shangri-La, the Montien and the Hilton International. Room prices start at US$50 and surcharges of up to 20 percent are added. Cheap accommodation such as youth hostels and guest houses can be found along Koh San Road, in Banglamphu, for as little as US$6.

ENTERTAINMENT

Bangkok's nightlife has something to offer everyone, with restaurants, bars and nightclubs to cater to every taste. Hundreds of restaurants are dotted round the city, offering all types of food at all types of prices. Hotel restaurants are more expensive but you can get a Thai meal in one of the smaller restaurants for a very reasonable price. Thai cuisine contains chili and is some of the hottest food in the world, though mild dishes are available too. If you are new to spicy curries and chili-based meals, then it would be wise to get used to the mild options first before trying your luck with the native hot dishes. Western food is also widely available and there is even a chain of McDonald's in Bangkok. Bars are also scattered around the city. The liveliest area and one of Bangkok's most famous is Patpong, where bars and markets stay open until the early hours. There are a number of movie theaters in Bangkok where films are shown either in English or in Thai with English subtitles.

ROLE OF INTERPRETERS

English is fairly widely spoken in Bangkok, particularly by the younger generation. However, the quality of written and spoken English varies greatly and careful consideration should be given to the use of interpreters before entering into any business negotiation. For simple deals it is not necessary for you to have your own interpreter at your side, as the Thai businessman will speak some English or can provide someone who can. But for more complex or weighty negotiations, an interpreter, preferably *your* interpreter, is needed. For one thing, an interpreter in your hire should give you an accurate interpretation of everything that is being said. For another, your arguments can be conveyed accurately. In fact, even though many senior executives of Thai companies have fluency in English, some prefer to conduct business negotiations with the help of a translator — official or unofficial — for similar reasons. It allows extra time to think and allows the Thai businessman to concentrate on the business at hand, rather than worrying about his language skills.

Other European languages are not commonly spoken by the Thais, so a European, for example, must converse in English or hire a translator. Publications, documentation and contracts written in English are more widely available than they were a few years ago, but in some smaller companies, this may not be the case.

WRITING IT ALL DOWN

Trading in Thailand follows international standards and a written contract is the universally accepted basis for any transaction. The contract provides — or should provide — an irrefutable reference point for all parties. It also provides an "insurance policy" to handle matters if things go wrong, i.e., an arbitration clause. Only the most traditional Thai supplier could interpret an insistence on a written agreement as a lack of trust. Arbitration clauses are now a normal, accepted part of international trade with no inference as to honesty or trust, and the seller is protected as much as the buyer.

EMBASSIES ABROAD
Thai Diplomatic Missions Overseas

Argentina
Royal Thai Embassy
Virrey del Pino 2458-6 Piso
1426 Buenos Aires
Argentina
Tel: 785-6504, 785-6521, 785-6532
785-6548

Australia
Royal Thai Embassy
111 Empire Circuit
Yarralumla
Canberra
Australia, A.C.T. 2600
Tel: 731-149, 732-937

Austria
Royal Thai Embassy
Weimarer Strasse No. 68
1180 Vienna
Austria
Tel: (0222) 348361, 318989

Belgium
Royal Thai Embassy
2 Square Du Val De a Cambre
1050 Brussels
Belgium

Tel: 640 6810, 640 6963
640 7071

Brazil
Royal Thai Embassy
Lote 10 Sector de Embaixadas Norte
Avenida das Nacoes Norte
P.O. Box 10-2406
70 433-Brasilia, DF.
Brazil
Tel: 24-6943, 244-7943

Canada
Royal Thai Embassy
85 Range Road, Suite 704
Ottawa, Ontario
Canada K1N 8J6
Tel: 37-1517

People's Republic of China
Royal Thai Embassy
No. 40 Kuang Jua Lu
Beijing
People's Republic of China
Tel: 521-903, 522-282, 521-748
521-867

Denmark
Royal Thai Embassy
Norgesmindevej 18
2900 Heller Up
Copenhagen
Denmark
Tel: 01-62-5010, 01-61-01-11

The Arab Republic of Egypt
Royal Thai Embassy
2, El Malek El Afdal Street
Zamalek, Cairo, A.R.E.
Tel: 801-356

France
Royal Thai Embassy
8 rue Greuze
75116 Paris
France
Tel: 704-3222, 553-5895
Tel: (0228) 355065, 351085

Hong Kong
Royal Thai Embassy
221-226 Gloucester Road
2/F, Hyde Centre
Causeway Bay
Hong Kong
Tel: 574-2201-4

India
Royal Thai Embassy
57-N, Nyaya Marg
Chanakyapuri
New Delhi 21
India
Tel: 615-985, 77089

Indonesia
Royal Thai Embassy
74 Jalan Imam Bonjol
Jakarta
Indonesia
Tel: 343-762, 349-180

Italy
Royal Thai Embassy
ia Nomentana 130

001 62 Rome
Italy
Tel: 832-0729, 832-0731

Japan
Royal Thai Embassy
14-6, Kami-Osaki 3-chome
Shinagawa-ku
Tokyo
Japan
Tel: 441-1386, 442-6750, 447-2247
 441-387, 441-7352

Kenya
Royal Thai Embassy
P.O. Box 58349
Nairobi
Kenya
Tel: 62742/3/4

Republic of Korea
Royal Thai Embassy
House 133, Namsan Village
Itaewon-ong, Yongsan-Ku
Seoul
Republic of Korea
Tel: 792-3098, 793-1301 ext. 708

Kuwait
Royal Thai Embassy
Jabriya Block 10, Area 12
P.O. Box 66647 Bayan
Kuwait
Tel: 314-870, 317-530-32

Malaysia
Royal Thai Embassy
206 Jalan Ampang
Kuala Lumpur
Malaysia
Tel: 488-222, 488-350, 488-420

Mexico
Royal Thai Embassy
Paseo de la Reforma 635
Lomas de Chapultepec 1 1000
Mexio D.F.
Tel: 520-1872

Netherlands
Royal Thai Embassy
Buitenrustweg 1
2517 K D The Hague
The Netherlands
Tel: (070) 452088, 459703

New Zealand
Royal Thai Embassy
2 Burnell Avenue
P.O. Box 2530
Wellington 1 New Zealand
Tel: 735-385, 735-391

Nigeria
Royal Thai Embassy
1, Ruxton Raod Ikoyi
P.O. Box 3095
Lagos, Nigeria
Tel: 81337

Pakistan
Royal Thai Embassy
23, Street No. 25
Shalimar 6/2
Islambad
Pakistan
Tel: 23992, 23974, 23991

Philippines
Royal Thai Embassy
107 Rada Street
Lagaspi Village Makati
Metro Manila
Philippines
Tel: 815-4219, 815-4220
        815-4221

Poland
Royal Thai Embassy
02-516 Warsaw
Staroscinska 1B, Apt. 2,3
Polish People's Republic
Tel: 492655, 496414, 494730

Portugal
Royal Thai Embassy
Avenida Almirante Gago Coutinho 68

1st Floor, 1700 Lisbon
Portugal
Tel: 805-359, 805 361

The Kingdom of Saudi Arabia
Royal Thai Embassy
North-East of Fly-over Sitteen Road
Near Al Eqtessad Est.
Makkarona Road
P.O. Box 2224, Jeddah

Singapore
Royal Thai Embassy
370 Orchard Road
Singapore 9
Tel: 737-2158, 737-3372
        235-4175

Spain
Royal Thai Embassy
Calle del Segre
29 Madrid-2, Spain
Tel: 250-3872, 250-4450

Democratic Socialist Republic Sri Lanka
Royal Thai Embassy
29 Gregory's Road
Colombo 7
Sri Lanka
Tel: 597-406

Sweden
Royal Thai Embassy
Sandhamnsgatan 36 (5/F)
Box 27065
S-102 51 Stockholm 27
Swden
Tel: 672-160, 678-090

Switzerland
Royal Thai Embassy
Eigerstrasse 60 (3/F)
3007 Bern
Switzerland
Tel: (031) 46-2281, 46-2282

Turkey
Royal Thai Embassy
Cinnah Caddesi 61/5-6
Cankaya, Anakara
Turkey
Tel: 381-120, 391-929

Union Of Soviet Socialist Republics
Royal Thai Embassy
3 Ripkinsky Pereulok
Moscow , U.S.S.R.
Tel: 201 4893

United Kingdom of Great Britain and Northern Ireland
Royal Thai Embassy
29-30 Queen's Gate

London, SW7 5JB
Tel: 01-589-2834, 01-589-2944
01-589-2853, 01-589-7338
01-589-2857, 01-589-0173

United States of America
Royal Thai Embassy
2300 Kalorama Road, N.W.
Washington, DC 20008
USA
Tel: 667-1446, 667-1447, 667-1448
667-1449

Socialist Republic of Vietnam
Royal Thai Embassy
So Nha E 1
Khu Ngoai Giao Doan Trung Tu
Hanoi, Vietnam

VIETNAM

A WESTERNER'S FIRST impression of Vietnam will probably be that this is a poor and backward country. He will most likely board his flight to Vietnam in Bangkok, Kuala Lumpur, or some other gleaming, computerized airport, and disembark at Noi Bai or Tan Son Nhat where there are no computers in evidence, and not much gleams in these 1950s-style facilities — apart from the friendly smiles of some of the personnel.

Although a few hotels feature modern communication and office equipment in their business centers, these are still the exception, and infrastructure remains a key problem for the businessman.

Educational levels are fairly high, with a literacy rate of nearly 90 percent, although the lack of knowledge of English, or any other foreign language, is a common problem.

VISAS

All foreign visitors to Vietnam require visas issued by a Vietnamese embassy. Both business or tourist visas are available. They are usually valid for a one-month stay and can be renewed within Vietnam.

Persons with letters of sponsorship can obtain visas on arrival at the airports at Hanoi or Ho Chi Minh City. The cost of these visas is said to be about US$25, but varies depending on the nationality of the visitor. Filling in the appropriate forms can take time, and a large number of passport-sized pictures is also required. It is generally simpler and more convenient to obtain a visa before arriving in Vietnam.

Since there have been cases of individuals being detained or otherwise inconvenienced as a result of not having the appropriate visa, it is best to obtain a business visa if actual deals are likely to be negotiated. On the other hand, if a trip is one of fact-finding and exploring the possibilities of doing business in the country, tourist visas are probably appropriate.

In countries or territories where there is no Vietnamese diplomatic representation, visas can be obtained through travel agents specializing in tours of Vietnam, or by submitting an application by mail to the nearest Vietnamese embassy abroad. Citizens of the United States might apply, for example, at the Vietnamese embassy in Canada, or through any travel agent handling tours to Vietnam.

Visas for investors

According to Vietnamese law, such entry visas, as a rule, are issued by Vietnamese diplomatic missions or consular offices in foreign countries not later than five days after the fulfillment of formalities for a visa application by the interested persons.

According to Vietnamese regulations, foreigners entering Vietnam to conduct investigations and preparations for an eventual investment may be granted multi-entry visas for a period not exceeding three months. Such visas may be extended for successive periods of three months each.

Foreigners participating in an investment project, including their personal assistants, may be granted multi-entry visas for a period not exceeding one year. This may be extended for successive one-year periods corresponding to the term of the contract, with due consideration of the length of time required for the process of dissolution of the enterprise or termination of the contract.

These visa provisions legally apply also to such foreigners' spouses, children, accompanying family members, and domestic helpers.

People obtaining visas under these conditions enjoy the right of "free circulation in areas deemed necessary for production and business operations, which have previously been registered to the State Committee for Cooperation and Investment."

Such foreigners may also circulate to other areas, the law says, if so authorized by the competent authorities concerned. This would probably be the police (security service) whom you could contact in your place of residence in Vietnam.

Besides this, you are of course, allowed to sightsee, but for this you would fall subject to the regulations of the General Department of Tourism.

It is important to note that Vietnamese law specifically excludes forbidden areas from any of the areas of free circulation, however. These forbidden areas normally include positions of strategic or military importance, where all foreigners are excluded, for reasons of national security.

There have been cases of foreigners being expelled from Vietnam on the grounds that they had travelled to areas where they had not been authorized to enter. Since it is quite easy to get permission to travel as a tourist throughout most of the country, there is really no excuse for getting into trouble over such issues. If from the beginning you "play it straight" with the authorities over such matters, you can count on being treated fairly, even indulgently, in return.

In urgent cases requiring an immediate solution to an unforeseen emergency or technical support to the investment project underway, a foreigner, may be issued an entry visa at the port of entry. But this is providing that a request to this effect is made by the authorized representative of the enterprise concerned or by the Vietnamese business partner. Such a request must be submitted to the State Committee for Cooperation and Investment (SCCI) 24 hours before the proposed entry.

AIR TRAVEL TO VIETNAM

Vietnam is rapidly developing its air links with the rest of the world. At the time of writing, there were direct air links between Ho Chi Minh City (where the runway is longer than in Hanoi) and the major foreign cities of Bangkok, Jakarta, Kuala Lumpur, Manila, Moscow, Paris, Phnom Penh, Prague, Singapore, and Vientiane. Direct service to Hong Kong is also just becoming available.

Among the air carriers which handle flights to and from Ho Chi Minh are Aeroflot (of the USSR), Air France, Garuda (of Indonesia), Thai International, Malaysian Air Service, Philippine Airlines, Air Laos, and Air Cambodia, as well as Vietnam Airlines (Hang Khong Viet Nam).

However, the vast majority of the 2,000 to 2,500 travelers arriving in Ho Chi Minh City every week are transit passengers from Bangkok as there is a daily service (about 13 flights a week) between Bangkok and Ho Chi Minh.

There are also three direct flights each week by Thai International between Bangkok and Hanoi, in addition to three runs by Vietnam Airlines.

Flights within the country are on the national carrier, Vietnam Airlines, which has been the frequent butt of jokes and criticism. Although much of the criticism has its justification — particularly as regards the fairly rudimentary cabin service — the airline is working to improve, and has made numerous attempts to acquire Western aircraft to augment its current fleet of Soviet-built airplanes.

However, the US embargo prohibits the sale to Vietnam of any products including US-made parts, and many aircraft, even those made by firms in Western Europe, incorporate engines or other equipment made in the United States. One European company unsuccessfully tried to go around the embargo by leasing, rather than selling, an aircraft to Vietnam, but this deal fell through due to US intervention.

Meanwhile, the prices of airplanes and spare parts from the Soviet Union have increased sharply as of the early part of 1991, when that country introduced international market prices in its deals with Vietnam.

As a result, Vietnam (strapped as it is for hard currency) faces considerable difficulty in maintaining its current airline service, let alone improving it. International interest in penetrating the Vietnamese market is likely to broaden the airline network servicing Vietnam, but mostly on the basis of increased flights by the airlines of other countries.

GETTING AROUND IN VIETNAM

Intercity travel within Vietnam had best be done by air, unless you have considerable time, or unless the distance separating the cities between which you are travelling is small. The rail system does link Hanoi to Ho Chi Minh City, but this is not a "bullet train", and its main advantage is its low cost.

Roads are reportedly in something less than optimum condition too. Still, the road network is fairly extensive, especially in the southern part of the country where the United States built many of them for strategic purposes in the 1960s.

Within the major cities of Hanoi and Ho Chi Minh, the street conditions are no worse than elsewhere in southeast Asia. In fact, in many respects, they are in far better condition since the volume of motor traffic on them is relatively limited.

There are no taxis, so if you are intent upon travelling by car you will need to hire one. This can be done most conveniently through your hotel and the standard price is US$50 per day, including driver. Naturally, you can also arrange with them just to take you to some particular place, or there and back, but make sure to agree with the driver on the price for such a trip ahead of time in order to avoid unpleasant altercations — and unexpected expenses — later. Although not many people speak much English, Vietnamese drivers are usually quite fluent in the language when it comes to bargaining with customers about prices.

The cyclo is the main alternative to the hired car unless you are determined to go on foot. Cyclos are tricycles with a rickshaw seat up in front. Cyclos, in fact, serve the function of taxis for Vietnamese society, and the local people make up the vast majority of their customers.

Still, cyclo drivers are, to say the least, eager to get the lucrative business of tourists and businessmen. They are far less costly than hired cars, but you will have to bargain with the driver to get the lowest possible price.

You can hail cyclos on the streets in Hanoi or Ho Chi Minh; in fact, cyclo drivers will often hail you if they see you on foot. There are usually clusters of cyclos and drivers waiting around hotel entrances as well, so these are by far the most accessible mode of transportation.

As in most large cities around the world, public buses also ply the streets in Vietnam. Generally well-worn and often crowded, the buses are at least inexpensive and the attendants on them will give you change when you pay your fare — a practice long abandoned in more "advanced" countries.

The attendants, one of whom is stationed by each door, also help riders to get on and off the vehicle. This service is especially important since bus drivers tend only to slow down, rather than fully stop, when letting passengers on and off.

One additional word of warning about buses, particularly those in Ho Chi Minh City, is that they regularly stop at bus terminals. During the five- or ten-minute interval they wait there, hordes of touts and beggars board and descend upon the passengers. Of course, if you are interested in reading a newspaper in Vietnamese or buying a trinket of dubious value, this is a convenient service, otherwise it could be seen as a nuisance.

Private cars in Vietnam are rare. Most traffic in the cities consists of trucks, buses, official or embassy cars, bicycles, and motorbikes. Bicycles by far predominate in Hanoi, while in Ho Chi Minh, the ratio of motorbikes to bicycles seems closer to 50:50.

The pedestrian in Vietnam should be aware that traffic signals are observed fairly regularly in Ho Chi Minh City, but much less so by the seas of bicycles in Hanoi. Also, at night, street lighting in both Hanoi and Ho Chi Minh City is fairly rudimentary — limited largely to the lamps hung out by the roadside shops and eateries that open after dark.

CLIMATE

Vietnam's climate varies considerably from the southern to the northern part of the country. This is particularly noticeable in winter, when Ho Chi Minh City will enjoy tropical summery temperatures of 33 Celsius (about 91 Fahrenheit), while the northern part of the country, including Hanoi, can experience windy and cold weather.

Vietnam lies in the southeast Asian intertropical monsoon zone, which is said to differ from similar monsoon zones in Asia. One way it is different is that it is subject to vigorous masses of polar air blowing south, producing a winter in northern Vietnam that is highly change-able, and which can be colder than in any other region at the same latitude. This zone is also distinguished for its high humidity.

On the other hand, in summer, temperatures are generally hot throughout the country, with average temperatures in the low 30s (degrees Celsius — around 90 Fahrenheit).

CLOTHING

Visitors to Vietnam must first of all be prepared for the varied climate if they come in winter. They would be well advised to bring summer clothing for Ho Chi Minh City, and sweaters and other warm clothes for their stay in Hanoi, where it is often cold, rainy, and where there is almost no indoor heating.

In summer, hot temperatures should be expected everywhere.

As far as the social requirements of dress are concerned, a suit and tie are expected for formal occasions, especially in the cooler weather of the northern winter.

In the summer, or in the hot weather of the south, a tie with a short-sleeve shirt should be quite sufficient, and dress, in general, is fairly informal.

ACCOMMODATION

Vietnam now boasts one five-star hotel, the Saigon Floating Hotel in Ho Chi Minh City. Equipped with conference facilities, a business cen-ter (with fax, telex, photocopier, personal computers, typing and secre-tarial services), two restaurants, bars, a discotheque, and numerous services, the Floating Hotel is unique in the country.

Other than the Floating Hotel, there are quite a number of hotels of an undetermined star rating — but with clean air-conditioned rooms with a private bathroom — in Ho Chi Minh and Hanoi. From the standpoint of the business visitor, their main drawback is the lack of modern communications facilities.

In Hanoi, in many cases the telephone in your hotel room is only capable of receiving calls. To call out, even within the same city, you need to go down to the lobby, or contact the hotel switchboard. Need-less to say, there are no such things as faxes or photocopiers in most Hanoi hotels.

However, there are many projects under way to build and upgrade hotel facilities in Vietnam. It is likely, therefore, that communications and business needs will be met very shortly, at least in some of the better hotels in Hanoi and Ho Chi Minh.

A selected list of hotels in Hanoi

> *State Guest House*
> *2 Le Thach*
> *Telephone: 55801, 55853*
> *Fax: 55855*

> *Thang Loi*
> *Yen Phu*
> *Telephone: 58211*
> *Telex: 411276*
> *Fax: 52800*

Hotel Thang Loi is Hanoi's premier hotel, apart from the State Guest House where newly-appointed ambassadors stay. Thang Loi even has a fax machine. However, it suffers from the drawback of being located way out of the center of town on the shore of a beautiful lake. It is a good location for holding meetings; bad if you have to go out and meet others.

The following Hanoi hotels offer similar accommodations but are more centrally located:

> *Dan Chu*
> *29 Trang Tien*
> *Telephone: 53323*
> *Telex: 411253*

> *Hoa Binh*
> *27 Ly Tuong Kiet*
> *Telephone: 53315, 54655*

> *Bo Ho*
> *1 Ba Trieu*
> *Telephone: 52075*

> *Hoan Kiem*
> *25 Tran Hung Do*
> *Telephone: 54024, 56547*

> *Thong Nhat*

15 Ngo Quyen
Telephone: 52785, 52787

A selected list of hotels in Ho Chi Minh City
Apart from the Tan Binh (Airport Hotel), all of the hotels in this list are located in Quan 1 — the city's 1st District (business district) — and all can be contacted by fax.

Saigon Floating Hotel
1A Me Linh Square, Quan 1
Telephone: 90783, 90624
Telex: 812614 HOTL
Fax: 90784

The Saigon Floating Hotel is the only five-star facility in the whole country.

Ben Thanh (Rex)
141 Nguyen Hue, Quan 1
Telephone: 92185/6, 93115
Telex: 811201, 812602 HOTBT
Fax: 91469

Bong Sen (Miramar)
117-119 Dong Khoi, Quan 1
Telephone: 91516, 99127, 20545
Telex: 811273/4
Fax: 99744

Cuu Long (Majestic)
1 Dong Khoi, Quan 1
Telephone: 91375/6, 95515, 23711, 23713
Telex: 811275/6 HOTCL
Fax: 91470

Doc Lap (Caravelle)
19 Cong Truong lam Son, Quan 1
Telephone: 93704/6/8
Telex: 811259, 812640 HOTDL
Fax: 99902

Hai Au (Continental)
132-134 Dong Khoi, Quan 1
Telephone 94456, 99201, 99255

Telex: 811344 HOCONT
Fax: 90936

Hai Van
69 Huynh Thuc Khang, Quan 1
Telephone: 91273/4
Fax: 91275

Huu Nghi (Palace)
56-64 Nguyen Hue, Quan 1
Telephone: 92860, 97284, 94722
Telex: 811208 HOTHN
Fax: 99872

Yuco
28-34 Nguyen Thi Minh Khai, Quan 1
Telephone: 95947, 98994
Telex: 811508 YUCO
Fax: 95947

Tan Binh (Airport Hotel)
201 Hoang Van Thu,
Tan Binh
Telephone: 41175, 41167, 41199, 44282
Telex: 811558 HOT TB

BUSINESS HOURS

Standard business hours throughout the country are from 7:30 in the morning until 4:30 in the afternoon, Monday through Friday, and Saturday mornings.

PUBLIC HOLIDAYS

New Year	1 January
Tet Lunar New Year	
(varies each year)	3-5 February
Emperor-Founder Hung Vuong	7 April
Reunification Day	30 April
May Day	1 May
National Day	2 September

FOOD AND DRINK

Vietnam offers a very wide variety of local food and drink at (in general) extremely reasonable prices. Vietnamese, Chinese, Continental European, and (to a limited extent) Indian and Japanese cuisine is available.

Vietnamese cuisine is similar to Chinese, but by no means identical with it. In general, it is said to be less sweet and less oily and features many unique delicacies. One distinctive aspect of today's Vietnamese food is that the local diet has thoroughly assimilated French bread. It regularly accompany meals and loaves are sold in little stalls all over the major cities.

There are so many Vietnamese restaurants representing all levels of quality in both Hanoi and especially in Ho Chi Minh that there is no need to offer a list of addresses here.

After dark, the established restaurants are augmented by street stalls (mostly selling noodles), and the numerous cafes — usually modest storefront establishments with a few stools and small tables. These have mushroomed in the *doi moi* years, since 1981, and most are privately run.

Chinese food is also available, particularly in Ho Chi Minh City, whose fifth district (Quan 5) was formerly known as "Cholon" or "China Town".

Western cuisine of sorts is available in major hotels and in some restaurants. Menus in Hanoi hotels tend to offer a rather limited variety, but they do make up for that in economy.

Many visitors to Vietnam who frequent roadside stalls and restaurants find themselves suffering from different types of gastro-intestinal complaints. There is no 100 percent guarantee against such problems, but the Vietnamese usually avoid unboiled water and it probably pays to follow their example in this. The traveler might also bring along some type of stomach medicine, just in case.

CURRENCY AND CREDIT

As at January 1991, the official exchange rate of the dong to the US dollar was dong 7,500:US$1. Unfortunately, the rate, which is set officially (but which reflects market prices fairly closely) was rising rapidly. This is bad news for the Vietnamese, who are quite worried about the inflation problem; but for the visitor to Vietnam, it means more dong for the dollar.

The banknote of the highest denomination issued in Vietnam is the

5,000 dong note. This means that if, for example, you change a US$100 note, you will get stacks and stacks of Vietnamese currency — three-quarters of a million dong — at least 150 banknotes. Fortunately, Vietnamese banknotes are small in size (the country has a lot of experience in inflation). Still, it will not be enough to just open your wallet — get ready to stuff your briefcase.

Also, bear in mind that many of the larger expenses, such as your hotel bill and hired cars, must be paid for in hard currency. Most of your other expenses will be in dong, but as prices in Vietnam are fairly low, you may not need too much local currency.

Also, Vietnamese currency regulations prohibit you from changing dong back into convertible currency. So, once you change dollars into dong, you are stuck with the dong. Also, technically, you are prohibited from taking dong out of the country when you leave.

There is no limit on the amount of currency you may bring into Vietnam. However, as in any country with a closed currency system, you are required to change money only at authorized places where you must get a receipt. Keep these receipts. When you leave Vietnam, you may be asked to show receipts to verify the spending of the foreign currency you declared when you entered the country.

Major credit cards are increasingly accepted in Vietnam, at least in major hotels and hotel restaurants in Ho Chi Minh. But they are still a very new phenomenon so never assume they are accepted. Hotel personnel in many of the smaller towns sometimes do not even know what credit cards are, much less accept them.

US law prohibits US citizens from using any credit cards in Vietnam, as this is regarded as a violation of the embargo and they are legally punishable when they return to the United States.

SHOPPING

Handicrafts and works of art are readily available in stores and shops in Ho Chi Minh and Hanoi. Vietnam is particularly well-known for its lacquer work and a wide variety of lacquered and inlaid pieces of furniture, boxes, vases, and the like.

Small woven carpets, handicrafts made of silver, porcelainware, paintings, tapestries, and other distinctly Vietnamese articles can be found in the many state-run shops catering to tourists.

Prices for all these goods are very low, making them very attractive to the Asian art fancier.

LANGUAGE

The most commonly understood language is Enlish, at least for simple purposes, although it is often said that many Vietnamese speak Russian or French.

Some individuals, to be sure, speak excellent French, particularly those of the older generation. Many professionals, such as doctors or engineers, have studied in the Soviet Union or Eastern Europe and speak Russian.

But among the general population, many speak a little English. That is, using English, you can probably get around, but any kind of in-depth conversations or negotiations will most likely require interpreters.

Some hotels provide interpreters, and most large state enterprises should have interpreters on their staff. Obviously, for in-depth detailed talks you might want to arrange for your own interpreter.

Considerable patience is also required when negotiations are going on through interpreters. Business negotiations routinely involve legal and technical matters where precision is of great importance. On the other hand, most Vietnamese interpreters graduate from some university language department, where they most likely studied philology, not business. So, they may not be fully conversant with the precise meanings of business jargon, legal terms, technical words, etc.

Therefore, make sure all final agreements are in writing, and do your level best to double check the translations. The quality of translated documents is much more reliable than that of verbal negotiations, but then the document you sign can have immense significance for your business.

The Vietnamese often say that when a contract is drawn up in two languages, both have equal legal validity. That may be. But if the translation of the document is faulty, any resulting legal disputes could still be highly complicated.

Generally speaking, the offices of the Vietnam Chamber of Commerce and Industry (VCCI) can help out with translations and their verification. Their staff is fairly conversant with trade terms.

BUSINESS CARDS

As in many other places throughout Asia, name cards are almost a prerequisite for work in Vietnam. If for no other reason, they facilitate communication, giving people a better idea of who you are, whom you represent, what you want and, indeed, how to pronounce your name.

TIME

In meetings with representatives of large firms, do not expect immediate answers and commitments. They will have to take your proposals and documents and digest them all, perhaps reporting on them to higher authorities, depending on whom you spoke with. Then they can get back to you with their own offers and decisions.

As noted above, even making appointments with trade representatives can take some time. Make sure you allow considerable time in Vietnam to arrange your business, since every step might entail unexpected delay. People will do their best to accommodate your schedule, but decisions and arrangements inevitably take some time. The country's infrastructural and communication deficiencies slow things down, as does the complication of bureaucracy.

OTHER TIPS

Australian businessman Ray Eaton, who has been doing business in Vietnam for several years, offered the following guidelines for foreign businessmen at an international conference in Hong Kong:

1. A foreign businessman must always recognize that he is a guest of that country he is visiting, or residing in, and must ensure that he strictly obeys the laws of the country.
2. If in doubt about the laws of Vietnam — Ask.
3. Register your arrival and departure with the police.
4. Do not travel around Vietnam without the correct travel permits.
5. Ensure that you enter Vietnam with the appropriate visa — do not conduct business activities in Vietnam if you have been issued a tourist visa.
6. Do not contact individuals who may have different political views to the government — remember, you are a businessman not an investigative journalist.
7. Do not carry any mail on behalf of third parties — you are legally responsible for the contents.
8. Do not take into the country any books, magazines, or newspapers with political content.
9. Do not become involved in smuggling. Not only are you endangering your own situation, but also creating additional problems for law abiding foreign businessmen.

VIETNAMESE CONTACTS ABROAD

Australia
Embassy of the Socialist Republic of
Vietnam
Commercial Section
6, Timbara Crescent O'Malley
Canberra ACT
Tel: 66509
Tlx: 62759

Britain
Embassy of the Socialist Republic of
Vietnam
12-14 Victoria Road
London W.8; R.D.
Commercial Section
12-14 Victoria Road
London W.8; R.D.
Tel: 9371912
Tlx: 887361

China
Embassy of the Socialist Republic of
Vietnam
32 Guanghua Lu
Jianguo Menwai
Beijing
Tel: 5321125, 5321155

Czechoslovakia
embassy of the Socialist Republic of
Vietnam
Holeckova 6
Praha 5
Tel: 546498, 531723
Commercial Section
V. Tisine 2 (Bulenec)
Praha 6
Tel: 121979

Egypt
Embassy of the Socialist Republic of
Vietnam
47, Noned Heshmet Street
Zamalak

Cairo
Tel: 3402401

France
Embassy of the Socialist Republic of
Vietnam
62-66 Rue Boileau
Paris 16e
Tel: 75016
Commercial Section
44, Avenue de Madrid
92200 Neuilly Sur Seine
Paris
Tel: 6248577
Tlx: 612922 SECOVIF

Germany
Embassy of the Socialist Republic of
Vietnam
37, Konstantin-Strasse
5300-Bonn
Tel: 0228, 3570201
Tlx: 8861122 SQVN

or

Embassy of the Socialist Republic of
Vietnam
1157, Berlin-Karlshor St.
Herman-Dunecker St. 125
Commercial Section
Clara Zetkin 97/111, 1080 Berlin
Tel: 229812
Tlx: 114237

Hong Kong
Representative of the National
Export-Import Corporations of the
Socialist Republic of Vietnam
17th Floor, Gol.den Building
20-24 Lockhart Road
Hong Kong
Tel: 5283361 (3)
Tlx: 63771 VNCOR HX

Hungary
Embassy of the Socialist Republic of
Vietnam
VI Benczurt. U. 18
Budapest
Tel: 429943
Commercial Section
24 Benczur Uha 1/1 Budapest VI
Tel: 420912
Tlx: 224590

India
Embassy of the Socialist Republic of
Vietnam
42 Floor, South Extension
New Delhi Part 1
Tel: 624586, 623823
Commercial Section
287 Defence Colony
110024, New Delhi
Tel: 698021

Indonesia
Embassy of the Socialist Republic of
Vietnam
25, Jalan Teuku Umar
Jakarta
Tel: 325347 M
Commercial Section
25, Jalan Teuku Umar
Jakarta
Tel: 3100358, 3100359
Tlx: 45211 SRVNAM

Italy
Embassy of the Socialist Republic of
Vietnam
Piazza Barberini 12
00187 Roma
Tel: 4755286, 4754098
Commercial Section
Pizza Barberini 12
00187 Roma
Tel: 4755286, 4754098
Tlx: 610121 VNROMAI

Japan
Embassy of the Socialist Republic of

Vietnam
50-11, Motoyoyogi-Cho Shibuya-Ku
Tokyo 151
Tel: 4463311, 4663312
Commercial Section
50-11, Motoyoyogi-Cho Shibuya-Ku
Tokyo 151
Tel: 4663325 (03)
Tlx: 32440

Malaysia
Embassy of the Socialist Republic of
Vietnam
4, Pesisan Stonor
Kuala Lumpur
Tel: 2484036
Fax: (603) 2483270

Mexico
embassy of the Socialist Republic of
Vietnam
Calle Sirra Ventawa, No. 255
Lomas De Chapultepec Delegacion
Miguel Hidalgo
Mexico D.F.
Tel: 5401612, 5401632

Philippines
Embassy of the Socialist Republic of
Vietnam
54, Victor Cruz
Malate, Manila
Tel: 500364, 508101

Poland
Embassy of the Socialist Republic of
Vietnam
00-468 Warszawa
Ul. Kawalerii 5
Tel: 413369, 415867
Commercial Section
Ul. Swiedtonkrzyska 36M-32
Warsaw
Tlx: 813908

Singapore
Representative of the National
Export-Import Corproations of the

Socialist Republic of Vietnam
10 Leedon Park
Singapore 1026
Tel: 4683747
Tlx: 33145, 388669

Sweden
Embassy of the Socialist Republic of
Vietnam
Orbyslotsvag 2612536 Alvsjo
Stockholm
Tel: 861214, 861418
Commercial Section
Parkvagen 42, S-13141 NACKA
Stockholm
Tel: (08) 7182841
Tlx: 15716, 10332

Thailand
Embassy of the Socialist Republic of
Vietnam
83/1, Wireless Road
Bangkok
Tel: 2517201, 2515836
Commercial Section
83/1, Wireless Road
Bangkok
Tel: 2517201, 2515836
Fax: (662) 2526950

Union of Soviet Socialist Republics
Embassy of the Socialist Republic of
Vietnam
Ulitsa Bol'shaya Pirogovskaya, 13
Moscow
Tel: 2500848
Tlx: 414411, 414321

The Importing Series

Inside tips and authoritative advice from Asia's largest trade publisher

Use our expertise to your advantage!

Anyone trading in Asia or around the world will benefit from the insights that **Asian Sources** can offer. After more than 20 years of helping people do business, we have a wealth of experience that buyers can depend upon.

Turn to our books first for expert, authoritative advice.

Importing from Asia successfully

This unique series of nine importing books features Asia's most dynamic markets... **Hong Kong, Taiwan, China, Korea, Thailand, Malaysia, the Philippines, India** and **Singapore**. Each book will provide you with an unrivalled knowledge of the business environment of the country. Take advantage of Asia's unique business opportunities with advice from experts who know these marketplaces inside out. You will find guidelines on:

- Local negotiating strategies
- Banking & finance
- Customs & culture
- Organizing shipping & payment
- Export regulations
- Alternative buying methods
- Investigating suppliers
- Trade terms & settling disputes

Explore the new markets

This new series of Importing books explores the emerging markets of **Vietnam, Czechoslovakia, Mexico, Poland** and **Mauritius**. Rising costs are making these new markets highly attractive to cost-conscious buyers. Each of these timely publications will help you to assess the risks and evaluate the benefits of importing from these countries. Don't "wait to see what happens" or you will miss profitable opportunities. These thoroughly researched publications will give you inside tips on:

- Doing business today—the pros & cons
- Recent events
- Products & investment opportunities
- Finding suppliers & negotiating tips
- Importing formalities & limitations

Negotiate with confidence

Get the best possible deals with the help of **Negotiating in Asia**. This invaluable reference book will give you the inside story on the cultural and practical aspects of doing business in each major Asian market.

THE **ASM** GROUP — Publications of The Asian Sources Media Group

To order, please complete the Order Form on the reverse page and send it, together with your payment to:
Books Dept, Asiamag Ltd, GPO Box 12367, Hong Kong • Tel: (852) 555-4777
or for faster service, FAX the Form to us on: (852) 870-0560

Book Order Form

Please enter the number of books you require below, together with the total price. Add US$5.00 per copy for air mail postage. **Air mail takes 7 to 10 days,** surface 5 to 7 weeks. We require that all details on this Form be completed in full, signed and dated.

Title	No. of Pages	Unit Price	No. of copies	Total Price
Importing from Hong Kong	229	29.95		US$
Importing from Taiwan	250	29.95		US$
Importing from the Philippines	198	29.95		US$
Importing from Thailand	194	29.95		US$
Importing from India	254	29.95		US$
Importing from Malaysia	226	29.95		US$
Importing from China	366	49.95		US$
Importing from Korea	252	29.95		US$
Importing from Singapore	194	29.95		US$
Importing from Vietnam	281	35.00		US$
Negotiating in Asia	116	29.95		US$
Tips for the Business Traveler in Asia	170	29.95		US$
Importing from Czechoslovakia	196	35.00		US$
Importing from Poland	200	35.00		US$
Importing from Mexico	306	35.00		US$
Importing from Brazil	–	35.00		US$
Importing from Mauritius	–	35.00		US$
Importing from Turkey	–	35.00		US$

Airmail ☐ Yes ☐ No   Please enter US$5.00 per copy | US$

Total | **US$**

Payment Instructions

- Payment should be made through US$ check or, preferably, US$ bank draft, drawn on a bank located in the US, made payable to **Asian Sources.**
- For telephone ordering or charging within the US/Canada, call Peg Mulder on (708) 475-1900.
- For credit card payment, please fill in your card details below and provide your signature.

1 **My check/draft is enclosed**

Check ✓ here please ▶ ☐

2 **I wish to pay by credit card**

Check ✓ here please ▶ ☐

Amount (US$)_____ ☐ ☐ VISA ☐ MasterCard

Card No └┴┴┴┴┴┴┴┴┴┴┴┴┴┴┴┴┘
Valid Until _____

Signature _____ Date _____

3 **Name** Mr ☐ Ms ☐ _____
Family Name   Given Name

Job Title _____

Company Name _____ **Div/Dept** _____

Street Address _____

City _____ **State/Province** _____

Country _____ **Zip/Postal Code** _____

Tel _____ **Fax** _____
Country Code   Area Code   Number   Country Code   Area Code   Number

Telex _____ **Cable** _____

4 Signature _____ **5** Date _____

Seven leading publications for importers of Asian-made products

THE ASM GROUP

Publications of The Asian Sources Media Group

FREE EXAMINATION ISSUE

Qualified readers may claim a FREE sample copy by completing the form on the reverse page in full or simply write us on your company letterhead.
Mail or FAX your sample request to:

Asian Sources Group of Trade Journals
Circulation Department, Publishers Representatives Limited
GPO Box 11411, Hong Kong • Fax: (852) 873-0488

Reserve your FREE sample copy now!

—Asian Sources magazines...essential sourcing tools for manufacturers & volume buyers—
Each magazine an undisputed industry leader

Asian Sources Electronics
- Audio
- Video
- Calculators
- Security Products
- Office Automation &
  Telecommunications
  section

Asian Sources Computer Products
Three sections:
- Computers &
  Peripherals
- Subassemblies/
  Manufacturing
- Media/Accessories/
  Supplies

Asian Sources Timepieces
Three sections:
- Watches
- Clocks
- Parts, Supplies &
  Equipment

Asian Sources Fashion Accessories
- Leather Goods
- Jewelry
- Umbrellas
- Footwear
- Sunglasses
- Hats
- Hair Care &
  Ornamentation
- Apparel &
  Manufacturing Supplies

Asian Sources Gifts & Home Products
- Furniture
- Household Goods
- Toys
- Gifts
- Premiums
- Sports, Health &
  Fitness Equipment
- Stationery for
  Office & Home

Asian Sources Hardwares
- Home
  Improvement &
  Builders' Supplies
- Hand Tools
- Power Tools
- Security Systems
- Automotive Parts &
  Accessories
- Industrial Supplies

Asian Sources Electronic Components
- Semiconductors
- Displays
- Resistors
- Capacitors
- Connectors
- PCBs
- Crystals
- Wire & Cable
- Test & Measuring
  Equipment

How to request a FREE sample
- Please write in the name of the magazine that interests you most (only <u>one</u> title).
- Answer questions **1** through **5** . Ensure you have signed and dated the form.
- Mail or fax your request to Circulation Dept, Publishers Representatives Ltd, GPO Box 11411, Hong Kong
  Fax: (852) 873-0488
- Allow a minimum 6 weeks to receive your FREE sample magazine.

✂ -

Please write clearly in BLOCK LETTERS **Sample Request Form**

☑ **YES!** Please send me a FREE sample copy.
I wish to receive **Asian Sources** _____ (only **one** title)
Magazine Title

Please answer all 5 questions below. We cannot send you a FREE sample copy unless ALL sections are completed.

Address Information

1 **Name** Mr☐ Ms☐ _____
Family Name / Given Name

Job Title _____

Company Name _____ **Div/Dept** _____

Street Address _____

City _____ **State/Province** _____

Country _____ **Zip/Postal Code** _____

Tel _____ **Fax** _____
Country Code / Area Code / Number

Telex _____ **Cable** _____

Business Information

2 **My job function can best be described as**   *Write letter here* ▶ ☐
Ⓐ Owner/Partner/Pres/MD   Ⓑ VP/GM/Dir   Ⓒ Mktg/Merchndse/Sales Mgr
Ⓓ Purch Mgr/Buyer   Ⓔ Eng/Prodn/Oper Mgr   Ⓕ Branch/Store/Dept Mgr
Ⓖ EDP/MIS   Ⓗ Other professional (please specify) _____

3 **Our primary business function is**   *Write letter here* ▶ ☐
Ⓐ Wholesaler   Ⓑ Distributor   Ⓒ Consultant   Ⓓ Retailer   Ⓔ Manufacturer
Ⓕ Agent   Ⓖ Other (please specify) _____

4 **Signature** _____ **5** **Date** _____

10BS10 ABS010/02

ASIAN SOURCES TRAVELER....
bringing you the latest in travel and business news from Asia!

TRAVELER will make your next business trip to Asia more profitable. By providing you with practical, up-to-date information on Asia, you can plan your schedule efficiently and get the most out of your business dealings. Each issue of **TRAVELER** covers:

- Destination report on Asian cities
- Making business contacts
- Business environment
- Good deals in transport, accommodation, dining, etc.
- Technology for traders

With **TRAVELER**, you will be informed and well-prepared for your next trip to Asia — giving you a competitive edge. You can concentrate on your business dealings in the region — confident that your valuable time is spent productively.

TRAVELER....especially designed to meet the travel needs of the Asian Sources reader.

**Publications
of The Asian Sources
Media Group**

GPO Box 12367, Hong Kong
Tel: (852)5554777
Fax: (852) 8730488

Malaysia,
A Fascinating
Destination

Fascinating
MALAYSIA

For more information please contact:
TOURIST DEVELOPMENT CORPORATION
OF MALAYSIA (Ministry of Culture,
Arts and Tourism)
P.O. Box 10328, 50710 Kuala Lumpur
Tel : (03) 2935188
Tlx : MA 30093 MTDCKL
Fax : (03) 2935884